PRAISE FOR *WE-COMMERCE*

"Throughout her career, Billee Howard has had a remarkable knack for positioning herself at the cutting edge of branding and understanding how new forms of media are changing the essential compact between producers and consumers of goods and services. In this book, she has once again nailed it. Relying on examples as diverse as honeybees and Andy Warhol, Howard makes a convincing case that producers and consumers are now linked in ecosystems in which the consumers don't just consume—they must help create products they are passionate about."

—William J. Holstein, international business journalist
and author of *The Next American Economy:
Blueprint for a Real Recovery*

"If you didn't read every blog and magazine about innovation in business these past few years, have no fear—just read Billee's book and she'll bring you up to speed! *We-Commerce* is your fast-track guide to making the most of the exciting era we are living in."

—Tammy Tibbetts, president and founder of
She's the First

"Billee Howard has created the ultimate handbook for how to do business in the sharing economy. Read it, learn from it, and put it to use before you wake up one day and find out your competitors have left you in their wake."

—Bob Davis, general partner at Highland Capital
Partners and former CEO at Lycos

"When it comes to brand-building in the digital age, Billee Howard is one of the savviest people around—and in *We-Commerce* she puts the lie to the notion that the most connected generation is somehow the most self-absorbed."

—Frank Rose, author of *The Art of Immersion* and
senior fellow at Columbia School of the Arts

"Billee Howard lays out a plan for finding new roads to success in the sharing economy through creativity, disruptive thinking, and collaboration. *We-Commerce* is a great tool for senior leaders to figure out how to place their brands at the epicenter of culture and commerce in ways that harness the power of digital storytelling to find new paths to profitability."

—B. Bonin Bough, chief media and ecommerce officer at Mondelēz International

WE-COMMERCE

WE-COMMERCE

How to Create, Collaborate, and Succeed in the Sharing Economy

BILLEE HOWARD

A Perigee Book

PERIGEE
An imprint of Penguin Random House LLC
375 Hudson Street, New York, New York 10014

Library of Congress Cataloging-in-Publication Data

Names: Howard, Billee.
Title: We-commerce : how to create, collaborate, and succeed in the
sharing economy / Billee Howard.
Description: New York : Perigee Books, 2015.
Identifiers: LCCN 2015037701 | ISBN 9780399173622 (hardback)
Subjects: LCSH: Economics. | Entrepreneurship. | Sustainable development. |
Relationship marketing. | BISAC: BUSINESS & ECONOMICS /
Economics / General.
Classification: LCC HB171 .H833 2015 | DDC 658—dc23
LC record available at http://lccn.loc.gov/2015037701

First edition: December 2015

PRINTED IN THE UNITED STATES OF AMERICA

1   3   5   7   9   10   8   6   4   2

Text design by Spring Hoteling

I'd like to dedicate this book to the fantastic group of "honeybees" in my hive who helped me find the courage to creatively evolve both personally and professionally. Bev, Laura, Allyson, Jen, Randi, Christine, and Aunt Iris—in a word, thanks. I wouldn't be who I am today without you. And to Maddie: I carry your heart. I carry your heart in my heart.

CONTENTS

CONTENTS

INTRODUCTION:
THE HOUSE OF WE

Most of the time, change, especially global change, happens gradually—so gradually in fact that we barely notice that anything's different. Time passes, one day changes to another, but we don't usually notice the hands of the clock moving.

Once in a great while though, forces combine, and a cataclysmic shift occurs that changes everything about life. One day, dinosaurs roam the earth, dominating the food chain so effectively that they tower over the rest of creation with arrogance and ease. The next day, an asteroid hits, the Jurassic gives way to the Cretaceous, and 75 percent of all species become extinct in the blink of a geological eye.

As in the natural world, sudden cataclysms do occur in the culture and the economy. One moment, we were feeding ourselves and our families out of our own kitchen gardens, making everything we used by hand, and using our only currency—the ability to trade and share with our neighbors—in order to survive the long winters. The next moment, we found ourselves living in cities, working long hours far from home, and buying rather than making or sharing what we needed to survive. The things that had fueled us before—community, creativity, cooperation, and sharing—had completely outlived their usefulness. "Own your own" became the dream and the driving force of the age. The "me economy" had begun. And then the recession of 2008 occurred, and everything changed once again.

We are still living in the long tail of the Industrial Revolution. We still go to work in offices and factories and mills. We live in cities and suburbs, instead of villages. We purchase mass-produced goods, rather than fashioning our own tools, and we are still dealing with the isolation, alienation, lack of connection, and diminishment of the singular human hand and voice that mass production and industrialization ultimately brought about.

But all that is changing, and it's changing quickly. After the destruction of the 2008 global financial collapse, once again, culture and commerce turned on a dime, and nothing would ever be the same again. Today, we are standing amid the ashes; what once prevailed no longer functions, and new species are emerging.

The "I, Me, Mine" mind-set of the industrial era came to an end in the crash of 2008. In its place came an economy and a culture built on a reimagined version of our core American competencies: socialization, sharing, trust, purpose, passion, creativity, and collaboration. We are building an economy of We-Commerce and returning to our small-community origins, only now our village is global in scale.

It is now possible to stand in solidarity with people on the other side of the world because of an idea, and for one person to launch a handmade innovative product and compete with big brands for the global customer's attention, loyalty, and consumer dollars. This means that not only the rules of the road to profitability but also the very definition of success itself has changed. A new success story is being told, with a whole different set of characters and plot twists, and with a reinvented vision of what the American Dream actually means.

Today, we are living in the economy that Andy Warhol foresaw decades ago. Fifty years after the introduction of the Factory, Warhol's idea of blending art with commerce and beauty with business is coming to fruition. In this book you will learn how to succeed in this rapidly shifting marketplace where culture and commerce are colliding like never before. I will offer you the insight you need to become a true artist of business and to introduce creativity into everything that your brand produces. I will show you how to obey the new laws of creative Darwinism, which favor the welfare of the we over the interests of the me.

As a communications specialist operating at the forefront of business for over two decades, I can interpret the changes that we see happening all around us and help you understand the new laws of the jungle. In *We-Commerce* you will learn how to transform your business model so that you are in step with today's key business mandates:

- Do it together for the good of the many and not just the few.

- Maintain a handmade, one-of-a-kind approach.

- Profit with purpose and meaning and inspire purpose in your communities and your employees.

- Grow big but think small.

- Use creativity and artistry as business competencies.

- Tell stories that engage us with ourselves and with others who share the same passions and interests.

- Bridge the physical and digital worlds.

We are living and working in a sharing-centered we-conomy, where the first rule for how to succeed in business is to understand that now, more than ever before, united we stand and divided we fall.

1.

Embrace the Awesome Power of Redemptive Deconstruction

I was on a business trip in Rome the day the financial markets collapsed in the autumn of 2008. Walking past the remnants of a once-mighty hegemony that ruled as the world's only superpower for five hundred years and contemplating the disaster back at home, I was struck by the interconnectedness of failure and success. There is a beautifully symbiotic relationship between destruction and redemption—one end of the spectrum enhances the other, like a pendulum that swings equally in both directions. In other words, you don't get a Renaissance without going through the Dark Ages.

Most people don't realize, but it actually took Rome a long time to fall. It lingered, sputtering along for decades as best as it could, refusing to relinquish its daily routines, its familiar symbols and structures, even though it was clear to the rest of the world that the empire was officially over. Finally, the barbarians at the gate (literally) forced the Romans to face facts by completely obliterating the last vestiges of that culture. They brought total devastation, and in so doing, paved the way for redemptive deconstruction.

Once ancient Rome was reduced to ashes, and not before, a new culture was able to spring up out of the void. From the Vatican to Versace, gradually, Rome began to redefine itself as a world power of a different kind. I found this a comfort as I contemplated what would rise up out of the rubble of the ruined U.S. economy and how we would retain the essence of what is best about our tried-and-true institutions while building up new structures and models that are completely different from anything we have ever experienced. This is the power of redemptive deconstruction, and it is happening all around us, and transforming the global marketplace at a rapid pace. Rome today *is* being rebuilt in a day, and thanks to the new rules of We-Commerce, all of us have the opportunity to participate in the creation of our new, shared citadel together, because the old rules of hierarchy, and might is right, have been swept away.

THE CRASH OF 2008:
THE GOOD, THE BAD, AND THE EVEN BETTER

Unlike in the tech bust of the late 1990s, we experienced more than just a U.S. stock market freefall in 2008. This time, every man, woman, child, company, government, and country felt the fallout. This was a market apocalypse. The damage was not limited to investors blinded by the rich promises of technology and soaring IPOs like Lycos, Pets.com, and Kosmos. It wasn't just drained brokerage accounts and bankrupt corporations littering the landscape and dragging our stock market indices down. This time, the collateral damage was personal: stolen life savings accounts, foreclosed homes, broken families, and shattered American Dreams. In essence a reset button was pushed, and the world began a total reboot after which our collective operating system would never work quite the same way again.

As we emerged from the fog of 2008, a number of big changes to the landscape became clear, which are transforming forever the way that we do business. We have learned some important lessons from the fall, and the new structures and systems that are taking hold are poised to make us a better society and a better economy in the long run. All we have to do is look back in history to realize that shifts of this magnitude result in giant steps forward that we might not have taken without the power of redemptive deconstruction.

WE-COMMERCE

Miracles of Redemptive Deconstruction:
The Model T Ford

I will build a car for the great multitude. It will be large enough for the family, but small enough for the individual to run and care for. It will be constructed of the best materials, by the best men to be hired, after the simplest designs that modern engineering can devise. But it will be so low in price that no man making a good salary will be unable to own one—and enjoy with his family the blessing of hours of pleasure in God's great open spaces.

—Henry Ford

The introduction of the Model T Ford in 1908 followed one of the most devastating stock market crashes of all time. The Panic of 1907, also known as the Banker's Panic, was a financial crisis that primarily affected bankers but sharply depressed the entire American manufacturing sector for a full year. The stock market fell nearly 50 percent from its peak in 1906, and there were numerous runs on banks and trust companies. Its primary cause was a credit crunch that began on Wall Street and soon spread across the nation, leading to the closings of banks and businesses.

This cataclysmic event, similar to the 2008 catastrophe, did not just demonstrate the failure of an individual or institution but symbolized the failure of a whole way of doing things. The Banker's Panic also hit a reset button for the country that would alter the world by introducing a brand-new industrial model that would come to define America: the assembly line. This reimagining of manufacturing provided a road out of the ruins and introduced the iconic "Tin Lizzie" to the world.

The Tin Lizzie, as an adoring America nicknamed the Model T Ford, was designed to be a practical, affordable vehicle for the average American family. Assembly-line production allowed the price of the touring car version to be lowered from $850 in 1908 to less than $300 in 1925. At an affordable price point like this, the Model T soon became the market leader, representing as much as 40 percent of total car sales in the United States.

The Model T helped chart an indelible course for America, and for Ford—one that would cement Henry Ford's reputation as one of the greatest innovators of all time and ensure the company's enduring legacy as one of the most revered automobile companies in the world.

THE NEW GOLDEN RULES

Today, the world must clearly understand that together we rise and together we fall. As the Lehman collapse and the cascading global financial destruction that followed demonstrated, we may all be separate, but we are also all connected in ways never before imagined. As such, the old ways of doing things no longer work. We cannot just continue on with the same set of failed rules and hope for a better tomorrow.

New world orders call for new rules of business. Here is the road map that I have developed to help you navigate this newly created and largely uncharted business landscape, retain the best of the old model, and innovate your way to success in today's we-conomy.

 New Golden Rule 1

CREATE A BRAND CULTURE THAT
ENCOURAGES TRUST AND SHARING

As we have discussed, in the new we-conomy shared experiences trump individual possessions time and time again. So much so, in fact, that a subsect of the overall collaborative economy has emerged. The rental and Netflix economy is thriving. Why? Because in a We-Commerce world, people are more focused on the experiences they can enjoy collectively as opposed to the material possessions they can stockpile individually and enjoy in isolation.

The seeds of this trend were all sewn with the rise of Airbnb and Uber as major industry forces. This global phenomenon of sharing and trust as a platform for the exchange of goods and services has not only shifted the face of industry, it has forever altered the face of commerce. Today, success is predicated upon providing new ideas and offerings based on that socially cooperative platform. In today's we-conomy, the road forward involves pooling our resources to build not just new products but new conceptual models of how our brand communities can interact and exchange ideas, products, and services with one another. Today, consumers want to deal directly with one another whenever possible and to get the middleman out of the way.

And so, as with Airbnb and Uber, this means creating a platform or a brand culture that facilitates trust and sharing between your community members and then getting out of the way and letting your consumers do the talking and the buying and selling, without anyone really knowing that you are there.

Airbnb

Airbnb is one of the pioneers of redemptive deconstruction that has turned the ideas of trust and sharing into a multibillion-dollar brand. Started by a Rhode Island School of Design (RISD) graduate who decided to rent out his own room to make ends meet, Airbnb has singlehandedly reimagined the global hotel and hospitality sector without even owning a single bed! Through the clever creation of a novel collaborative commerce model, Airbnb has ushered in a new worldwide economic ecosystem of sharing that is making ownership a thing of the past.

Airbnb understood that in a post-2008 world, we are now more connected to each other than ever and also more skeptical of big brands. We are, therefore, less inclined to depend on big brands to assess and supply our needs and more inclined to rely on each other. Brian Chesky realized that if someone created a trust platform that brought guest and innkeeper together without a middleman, huge value could be created for both parties, and also for his own brand.

This was Airbnb's real innovation—creating a network of trust in which everyone could not only learn about their hosts in advance but then rate their experience afterward, and all without big brand intervention. This meant everyone using the system would pretty quickly develop a relevant reputation, visible to everyone else in the system and reliably authentic because it is generated by the people and for the people.

Uber

Uber is another example of redemptive deconstruction creating a new model out of the remains of the old, based on trust and sharing. Uber didn't invent the idea of affordable car service. Car services have been around since the beginning of time—or cars. But Uber, like Airbnb in the hospitality sector, created a new kind of service, based on resource sharing. Uber allows anyone with a car to become a driver and anybody who needs a lift to access a car service on demand. As in Airbnb, drivers and users rate each other, thereby establishing a reliable system of measurement that establishes trust. Uber, however, offered another element, which was to make a luxury service formerly reserved for the affluent available to all.

Uber, a company that is only six years old, is now valued at $41 billion, grander in market cap than the likes of both Burger King and Dunkin' Donuts combined. Why? Because Uber didn't seek to compete with an existing product or service or to simply make something that exists slightly better. They completely changed the game and leveled the playing field in a formerly vertical luxury space by harnessing customers' appetite for doing business within a community of individuals whom they know and trust.

 New Golden Rule 2

BE A REDEMPTIVE LEADER

In order for your organization to harness the power of redemptive deconstruction, there must be top-down support for the characteristics required to be successfully disruptive. This means that you need to cultivate leaders who are driven to disrupt at every stage in the supply chain. What you make, how it is made, where it is made, and how your customers are serviced—all should be open for reinvention. Redemptive leaders understand this and act on it.

In addition, learn how to inspire faith and hope within your team as well as within your brand communities. Faith is one of the most powerful tools in a CEO's arsenal today, so use it for the good of the whole. Possessing unshakable faith, inspiring that quality of belief in others, and transforming that passion into believable hope are among the most critical strategic imperatives of corporate leadership.

Disruptive Leadership on the Front Lines: Alan Mulally and One Ford

Among the greatest examples of leadership in the sharing economy that have emerged post-2008 is Alan Mulally, who was the CEO of Ford Motors until June 2014. Mulally, the former CEO of Boeing, was called in to breathe new life into one of the sputtering big three giants amid the world's economic collapse, and he did so by inspiring belief through the pure charismatic force of his optimism.

Mulally, a man who had spent his career imagining the future of air travel, had seemingly none of the correct experience required to transform one of the largest car companies in history. Yet he came in and did just that. Why was he able to do this? Because he knew that imagining the future of the U.S. auto sector had little to do with cars and lots to do with aspiration and belief. He knew the future of Ford depended on rekindling the belief among employees, dealers, investors, suppliers, and communities that Ford was making the best and could become even better!

To accomplish this, Mulally rebuilt the company around the concept of One Ford, which consisted of four main points, all of which worked together to ignite and sustain optimism and faith in Ford's future and everyone connected with creating it.

1. Bring all Ford employees together as a global team.

2. Leverage Ford's unique automotive knowledge and assets.

3. Build cars and trucks that people want, value, and believe in.

4. Arrange the significant financing necessary to pay for it all.

From any angle, this was a plan that required the company to fire on all cylinders—strategic vision, financial health, workforce competitiveness, and product development. No small task, but somehow Mulally's optimism inspired people to reset the bar for their personal bests, and collectively Ford reimagined their company and their industry, which had been teetering on the brink of collapse.

 New Golden Rule 3

RECOGNIZE THAT FAILURE IS THE NEW SUCCESS

Historically, failure has been a no-no—something to deny. Something to run from or hide at all costs. Wall Street never rewarded failure. In fact it punished it with battered earnings reports and falling stock prices. But in our post-2008 world, measured and strategic failure today lays the groundwork for tomorrow's most astonishing success stories. Businesses are realizing that failure is the greatest teacher and that embracing it is the best way to ensure future successes.

The majority of the causes of the 2008 financial contagion stemmed either from denial and an inability to admit failure or from hyperattenuated methods put in place to try to prevent failure at all—which is in itself a form of hubris that precedes the fall.

The lesson we can all take from this as business leaders is to openly acknowledge what works and what doesn't and to be brave enough to completely destroy what doesn't work in order to innovate a solution that works even better. Similarly, we can no longer afford, as businesspeople, to rest on our laurels when times are good and anticipate that everything that works today will continue to work tomorrow. With the ever-accelerating pace of change, what defines success today will very likely change more quickly than we can anticipate.

Good judgment comes from experience. And experience comes from bad judgment—from failures. So embrace failure, understand it as an important step in learning what enduring success looks like. And when failure happens, remember that the key factor is how you respond: whether you learn from it and rebound or self-destruct. And always remember that there is nothing more appealing than a good old comeback story.

Greatest Comeback Stories Ever Told: Hillary Clinton

Hillary Clinton is potentially the greatest modern example of failure becoming the new success. Clinton failed to win the battle for a presidential bid in 2008, but she won the war as she built on that failure to define her future fortune.

As secretary of state under the man who defeated her, Clinton blazed a trail for globalization. She demonstrated unprecedented knowledge of the emerging global market canvas that the administration missed, while also transforming herself into a vessel of expression for women everywhere.

Clinton showed us how the world was shrinking, and interpreted this change for mainstream culture as a positive, rather than a threat. Clinton's course correction from failed candidate to global leader is bringing women together to champion a better order. And today, she is pioneering a new kind of campaign politics, fostering relationships one person at a time and bringing the redemptively deconstructed ideal of small as the new big to national politics.

Whether you are building a personal brand or are a purveyor of products and services, Hillary Clinton provides an excellent example of how we can all use failure as a ladder to new and unimagined successes—by learning from our failures, by putting failure to use in our pursuit of success, and by inventing new models of prosperity.

New Golden Rule 4

CULTIVATE MAVERICKS AND ENCOURAGE
THEM TO BREAK THE RULES

The best source of innovation is to attract and retain innovative talent, which is vital for growth. This means finding and hiring talented mavericks and then placing them within a culture that rewards them for breaking the rules. So make it a point to target and reward the mavericks in your company for shunning conformity. This can be difficult for old-school brands that are in the practice of weeding out and discarding squeaky wheels because they impede progress. In an era of redemptive deconstruction, weeding out your mavericks is one of the most destructive things that you can do as a company. So learn to recognize who they are and place them at the center of your organization's success strategies.

Innovators today are not the traditional geeks or tech gurus we thought of back in the old days. Innovators and mavericks today come in as many hues as a bag of Skittles. Here are just a few examples of new generation mavericks:

- The **Challenger**, who criticizes outdated processes and products and pushes the envelope to imagine things that aren't just improvements but have never before been seen.

- The **Conscious Capitalist**, who calls out unethical or self-defeating practices and challenges the organization to always profit and perform with purpose.

- The **Anarchist**, who disagrees with the mantras of an organization and wants to reinvent corporate ethos.

- The **Tinkerer**, who ceaselessly dabbles with new models.

- The **Nonconformist**, who shuns the normal and the routine.

Milestone Maverick: Brian Chesky

Airbnb began with an air mattress. When maverick Brian Chesky and his friends were trying to figure out a way to make money, they decided to rent out their house to accommodate visitors who were in town for a local design conference and were shut out due to hotels being at capacity. They blew up air mattresses and served breakfast, and Airbnb was born. Today, thanks to Chesky's willingness to break the rules, that small house repurposed as an inn in San Francisco has spawned a community of thousands of properties globally, offering unique lodgings with which to enjoy and travel the world, with the help of the properties' hosts.

Whether it is a tree house in Vermont, a house Jim Morrison used to live in, a yurt in Mongolia, or a castle in the foothills of Scotland, Chesky's model offers a new vision of the modern travel experience because he had the courage to think about the tried-and-true in a radically different way.

 New Golden Rule 5

MAKE CHANGE A CORE BUSINESS COMPETENCY

In today's marketplace, your company's greatest asset, and only constant, is its ability to marshal the forces of change for its own benefit. This requires the courage to force yourself into an uncomfortable place, especially when things are going along smoothly. We must all recognize that the world and the market are changing at a pace more rapid than we have ever seen before; your competitors today will probably not be your competitors tomorrow, so adaptability and the ability to appropriately respond to change are the little-known factors driving much current success. This counter-intuitive idea of preparing for transformation even when you don't need to change in the moment is central to remaining successful and relevant in an evolving market-place.

Deconstruction Comes to Cable: HBO

HBO is the ultimate example of redemptive deconstruction in mass media. It challenged previously uncontested ideas about the television market by focusing on just one major goal: great quality demonstrated in the form of the most artful storytelling imaginable. This bold step ultimately led to a TV revolution in which content needed to be so good that it could draw an on-demand audience.

Believe it or not, there was a time when creating quality television content didn't make good business sense. In the three-network paradigm, the goal was always to generate programs that appealed to the broadest possible market. It was a model completely reflective of a time when business broadly adhered to these paradigms as well. Bigger was better according to the GE Six Sigma management gold standard of the day, which meant being good at as many things as possible, all at once.

Cable television slowly began to introduce a world that would edge toward more quality content designed to satiate a specific niche appetite. In doing so, the subscription model of content consumption began to lay the groundwork for much of the current popular on-demand content creation.

With HBO, fueled by subscribers, the idea of highly marketable niche content was born. HBO needed to create programming that people would like so much that they were willing to pay for it. It was that unique business model that made iconic hit series *The Sopranos* possible. But *The Sopranos* wasn't HBO's first original show. What it was, instead, was the first show that took the unique attributes of HBO programming and also became a hit. *The Sopranos* demonstrated that television could aim for high quality, keep audience loyalty, and be broadly popular as well, if it was done right. Every original series that came after on HBO, Showtime, A&E, FX, and the rest of the cable original-programming providers stems from that new and daring idea.

According to *Wired* the new HBO GO no-cable streaming service will be a breakout hit. This move without question positions the former cable titan—now a mobile studio giant—to compete head to head with Netflix and Amazon, in both original programming and mobility. With HBO's new streaming service HBO GO, we may very well be entering an HBO economy and saying Netwho? one day.

REDEMPTIVE DECONSTRUCTION REMINDERS

- Foster trust and sharing in your brand community.

- Be a leader who inspires belief and passion.

- Use failure as a road to newly imagined success.

- If the rules no longer apply, break them, and encourage your employees to do so as well.

- Consider change as an opportunity and a valuable tool, rather than an obstacle to progress and growth.

2.

Adapt to the Laws of Creative Evolution

There is perhaps no better example of creative evolution-ary success than the honeybee. Honeybees, along with a handful of other insects like ants, are the only super-socialized species on earth. They live in colonies, working together to provide for the whole society and never for the individual. It is literally one for all and all for one all of the time. Although this elite class represents only 2 percent of the number of insects on the planet, they have dominated all of the most desirable food sources, conquered their competitors, and today outnumber all other species of insects combined by weight. Colony insects learned that the best way to survive is to live with and for the good of the whole hive.

Of all of the super-socialized insects, honeybees are the most sophisticated. Their evolutionary success is not only responsible for their own survival but *our* own and that of many other species. Were it not for the honeybee's ability to pollinate, no flower or grain or animal that feeds on them would have ever come to prominence. But honeybees are more than just a successful engine of pollination; they took things a step further and became artists of business.

One of nature's well-kept secrets is that honeybees are great dancers. They use movement as their primary means of communication. Through intricate footwork, they can communicate what the hive needs to know and do in order to grow and endure. Honeybees have a dance to communicate directions to new food sources when the hive is hungry, they have a dance to communicate the way to a new home when the hive is in danger, and they have a dance that locates the source of a threat so that the hive is prepared to defend itself.

The dance of the honeybee is a shining example of the granular brilliance of creative evolution in motion. Natural selection in honeybees has favored those who are best at using their creative storytelling abilities to communicate a tale that allows for the success of the entire hive.

So what do the honeybees know about taking care of business that we don't? They know that in the long run, competing as a group results in greater success than competing as an individual. They know that when groups compete against groups, it is the most cohesive and creative teams that survive.

Today, when we are all as interconnected as honeybees in a hive and dependent on each other for success, we can learn a great deal from them. Successful businesses today are led by teams dedicated to the whole and in search of a higher value than pure self-interest. Further, successful companies are single-mindedly dedicated to the pursuit of creative communication and telling stories that are focused on increasing the productivity and harmony of the community.

DARWINIAN DISRUPTION

Honeybees and humans didn't always have socialized skills. Just as we diverged from a less cooperative species of earlier apes, the honeybee is evolutionarily related to the wasp, which does not function in a group and definitely cannot dance. Yet at some point, both humans and honeybees experienced a major transition that put such pressure on the species that they had to creatively disrupt themselves in order to survive.

This is what today's businesses are doing as well. In order to survive the transition from a production model rooted in the Industrial Revolution to a more global, community-focused economy, businesses have to learn how to think like honeybees. In today's business environment, a higher level of natural selection has taken hold, which favors not the strongest individual, but the most cohesive superorganism.

DARWIN'S BUSINESS

In today's business environment, self-interest is taking a back seat to group well-being. The whole is more important than the individual parts. Products, services, and business models that foster a culture where people work together for the good of the whole are now selected for we-volutionary success. And this means that businesses in the we-conomy favor different characteristics in their workers than in previous times. Those who are able to demonstrate altruism, self-sacrifice, cooperation, and team spirit are more successful than those who are able to command the biggest piece of the pie. The power of we has replaced the power of me. Companies today have to adjust to these new laws of group selection and creatively adapt themselves to be harmonious and cooperative group organisms in order to succeed.

THE LAWS OF CREATIVE WE-VOLUTION

There are new laws of the jungle to observe in order to ensure survival and success. By applying these new laws, you can position your business to prosper in an economy that now selects for the most effective group.

Law of We-volution 1
CONFRONT CHALLENGES WITH CREATIVITY

Just as the dance of the honeybees is central to the survival of the hive, creative self-expression is a critical business competency today. This is the understanding that creativity is not just a peripheral function relegated to your design department but should be distributed throughout your organization as a whole. Engage creativity from the first moment of every endeavor and place an emphasis on humanity in your business. These are the tools that will aid your company's evolution and produce the innovations that will lead you to newer and even more productive practices.

HOW EARBUDS CHANGED THE WORLD

When Steve Jobs brought on Jonathan Ive as head of industrial design for Apple he gave him one guiding and central instruction: Marry humanity with innovation. The human connection, Jobs explained, needed to be front and center in anything that Ive might imagine. The result was perhaps the finest example of creative Darwinism ever imagined—the lily-white earbud.

The white earbud reinvented one sector and created a whole new sector at the very same time. The annoying black and ill-fitting earpieces made infamous by the airlines were obliterated with the introduction of the Apple earbud, which at the time of launch was revolutionary despite the fact that it admittedly took its inspiration from less organic and comfortable technology invented for transistor radios. The earbud was not an earplug or a headset; it was a pod designed to seamlessly fit your ear in an unobtrusive way while simultaneously delivering the best music experience to date.

As if that weren't enough, the earbuds were white instead of black. And because they were white and designed to be noticed, they became as much a badge of cool as a utilitarian staple. Earbuds were as innovative and world changing as the iPod. By pairing a first-of-its-kind music player with an innovation in audio equipment, Apple started a sound revolution. Apple's white earbuds helped make sound mobile, but, more important, they created a billion-dollar industry based not only on earbuds or headphones but sound itself.

Law of We-volution 2

ACQUIRE, RETAIN, AND COMMUNICATE KNOWLEDGE

One of the greatest achievements of the honeybee is the ability to acquire and retain knowledge, and then to communicate that information to others. Worker bees learn about the location of food sources, scout out new ecosystems that will sustain them, identify the presence of danger, and then are able to communicate that knowledge to others through dance. The course of human evolution has also selected the best storytellers and the best listeners as the strongest survivors. The same is true for businesses today. The ability to understand the lessons of your business and tell a story that imparts this wisdom to others in your company—as well as your customers—is paramount to survival and success. Today's businesses must be able to learn, adjust, and then tell a story that inspires others to action.

THE CISCO STORY

A great example of a company learning from its mistakes and then telling a story that inspires others to action is Cisco Systems. Cisco has been an industry leader for decades in bringing the wireless world to life, but it stumbled a bit in the early 2000s after its well-respected CEO became a bit too boastful and overextended not only himself but his company. Cisco hit a real rough patch. Earnings fell, shareholder confidence waned, and the company lost its compass.

This is the moment when truly great companies have the ability to redirect the ship to calmer waters, by beginning a new narrative that inspires stakeholders to turn their sails and find their way to safer harbor. Cisco is one of those truly great companies.

Under the brave stewardship of the legendary John Chambers, Cisco admitted its missteps and began a new path forward based on collective leadership from within and a collaborative storytelling effort throughout that reenforced the connections between employees and customers. It is worth noting that over decades of executive churn and burn across the global business landscape, Chambers stands out as among the very few career-long CEO rock stars who remain standing to this day.

In 2001, Cisco went from being the most highly valued company in the world to a classic example of the danger of bubbles. In 2008, in the midst of wide economic free fall, the company had a cushion of $26 billion in available cash, two dozen promising products in the pipeline, plus a disruptive strategy called the "human network effect," which would effect radical change both on and off the Cisco campus.

To enact this enormous metamorphosis, Chambers boldly reorganized the entire corporate structure. Under the new mandate, leaders of business units formerly competing for power and resources would now share responsibility for one another's success. What used to be me was now we, said Cisco.

The goal was to get more products to market faster. Seven years later in 2015, the Cisco human network, powered by not just one great CEO but by many visionary leaders, is responsible for helping the world transform itself into an economic and cultural ecosystem of interconnectivity.

According to Chambers in the company's second quarter 2015 earnings report:

Our strong momentum is the direct result of how well we have managed our company transformation over the last three plus years and our leadership position in the key technology transitions of cloud, mobility, big data, security, collaboration, and the Internet of Everything. Every nation, every company, everything is becoming digitized and the network is at the center of this transformation.

It has become clear that the evolutionary story of the Cisco Human Network, "Tomorrow Starts Here," has become not just moniker but reality, all because of their ability to embrace change and fearlessly write a happier conclusion to their narrative.

Not only has their story inspired the success of countless leading companies but its human effect has encouraged a new generation of innovators. Here is how they tell the story of the Human Network Effect on the Cisco website:

The human network effect creates understanding, where once
there were walls. It connects a kid to a scientist to a CEO to save a glacier.
It brings ideas together. Passions together. And people together.
It's the human network effect. The effect that is changing the world.
When technology meets humanity on the human network, the way we work changes.
The way we live changes.
Everything changes.

Law of We-volution 3
DIVIDE LABOR DEMOCRATICALLY

Honeybees are artists of labor division, and what a bee does in the hive is determined before it is even born. It is a highly precise system, with worker bees, drone bees, and the queen all performing their necessary functions and co-creating a successful outcome, without giving any thought to hierarchy. They are all equally important to the hive and perform their functions enthusiastically and faithfully as a result. You will never find a drone asking to be a queen or vice versa. And interestingly enough, the personality of the queen impacts the personality of the entire hive.

In order to compete today, try to make innovation a democratic dialogue that is driven from the bottom up as well as from the top down. Co-create with your colleagues, employees, and consumers, and be sure to remind everybody in the hive that they are important by incorporating their creative ideas and stories from the beginning of the supply chain.

HOW THE PORSCHE CAYENNE PROVED THE EXPERTS WRONG

A great example of Creative Evolution in motion is the Porsche Cayenne, which the company co-created by asking their consumers to tell them what they would want if they owned a second Porsche. The goal was to turn the Porsche diehard loyalist into a multiple–Porsche family home. When Porsche asked its customers, they nearly unanimously said that they would want a Porsche luxury SUV, and hence the Cayenne was born.

Despite the select few influencers who used to rule opinion in the auto industry, saying that an SUV was the complete opposite of what buyers wanted in a newly green-focused world, Porsche went ahead with its plans. They shunned the opinions of the few for the creative insights of the many. The result? The Cayenne is not only one of the best-selling SUVs on the market today but is also one of the greatest successes in Porsche history.

Law of We-volution 4

EVERY INDIVIDUAL IS IMPORTANT

The honeybee knows that it must protect and sustain every member of the colony because every individual is important to the survival of the hive. It's imperative to realize that every member of your business ecosystem, from employees to consumers, is essential to your survival, and none is more important than another. As a result, if you want to create a winning business today, you have to create for the benefit of yourself, your employees, and your shareholders but also for the benefit of the whole colony—the world around you. People today will gravitate to your products or services more often if you are giving back to the ecosystem that supports you and to the people who sustain you.

TOMS' WIN–WIN MODEL

TOMS Shoes was founded to actualize the one-to-one business model its founder Blake Mycoskie imagined. The idea was to create a company that would make shoes to make a profit but also to help those in need.

In 2006, Mycoskie befriended children in a village in Argentina and saw that they didn't have adequate shoes to protect their feet. Wanting to help, he created TOMS Shoes, a company that would match every pair of shoes purchased with a pair of new shoes for a child in need. The principle was called One for One. In 2011, the One for One model was expanded and TOMS Eyewear was launched. With every pair of TOMS glasses purchased, TOMS helps restore sight to a person in need.

What began as a simple idea to give back to a community and combine profit with purpose has evolved into a powerful business model helping address need and advance health, education, and economic opportunity for children and their communities around the world, while still making a profit and sustaining their own business colony. TOMS Shoes clearly demonstrates the power of creative we-volution at

> work: Since 2006, TOMS has put ten million pairs of shoes on children's feet in over sixty countries. And since 2011, TOMS has restored the sight of over 150,000 individuals through purchases of TOMS Eyewear.

Law of We-volution 5
REMAIN VIGILANT TO EVERY CHANGE

Honeybees never sleep. A beehive is an active factory of success 24 hours a day, 7 days a week, 365 days a year. This is not to suggest your business never close or take a break. There are forty thousand bees in an average hive, so they can rotate out workers and take shifts. The important take-away is that bees have devised a system that allows them to remain perpetually aware of their environment and respond to it instantly, all of the time.

One of the most critical components of our creativity driven economy is its mercurial nature. People constantly discuss the twenty-four-hour news environment. No one, however, discusses the 24/7 creation environment. In a world that never turns off, where technology democratizes creation and gives everyone the same opportunity to become an artist and change the culture rapidly, it is not the pace of commerce that you need to be most aware of but the pace of culture and creative output.

A world where everyone sleeps when you do no longer exists. Creativity is relentless and the brands that dominate the marketplace of tomorrow will be those that never let up and continually find ways keep up with the pace of the culture.

THE RAINBOW-STUFFED OREO

Kraft Foods has done an excellent job of staying in touch with the relentless pace of culture and realizing growth and brand impact as a result. One example is the now famous rainbow-stuffed Oreo, which appeared on the Oreo Facebook page during gay pride month, along with the caption "Proudly support love!" Within seventeen hours more than 157,000 people had liked the image, 40,000 people had shared it, and 20,000 commented. While Kraft had no intention of ever marketing the rainbow-stuffed Oreo, it nevertheless put the brand at the center of what was happening in culture at that moment, using the Oreo as a canvas to make and interpret history.

Another stellar example of the way in which Kraft has used the Oreo as a conduit to culture is the award-winning Dunking in the Dark campaign, which took advantage of an unexpected power outage during the Super Bowl. Because Oreo had a mission control set up for the express purpose of responding in real time to anything that might happen during the game, Oreo was able to capitalize on the unexpected blackout with the tweet "you can still dunk in the dark." The Dunk in the Dark image was shared on Twitter and Facebook more than 20,000 times and garnered 525 million media impressions, which is five times as many people as tuned in to watch the game!

Law of We-volution 6
SEARCH FOR NEW MARKETS AND RESOURCES

A honeybee colony will fly a total of around fifty thousand miles to make just one pound of honey and can travel as far as five miles away from the hive in search of resources. If they stuck to familiar ground close to home, they would likely not survive when food becomes depleted, circumstances change, or the hive becomes overpopulated.

Similarly, when you're looking for the next big creative inspiration, let the bees remind you that searching in traditional places will probably not produce the most honey. While you may not need to physically fly tens of thousands of miles, you can let your curiosity and your imagination wander to discover new resources to enrich your business. These days, creativity is increasingly coming from every nook and cranny of the globe, and identifying and developing new pockets of innovation are critical to sustainability and success.

A NEXT-GEN WARHOL TAKIN' IT TO THE STREETS

As in Warhol's day, the art world is now experiencing a disruptive renaissance, moving out of the galleries and into the streets, alleys, and back lots of the world and in the process, inspiring a whole new generation audience that looks very different from the gallery goers of yesteryear.

Artists like Banksy are challenging everything we thought we knew about what is and is not art and, in doing so, are giving us a great lesson about how to generate growth by traveling long distances in search of new markets, without looking any farther than our own back alley.

When Banksy came to New York City in 2013, he launched a series of guerilla art attacks on the edifices of neighborhoods all over Manhattan. He worked only at night, and in the morning, people would scour all five boroughs to discover his latest masterpiece. Banksy's street art interacts sometimes playfully, sometimes sardonically and philosophically with the familiar structures, signs, and symbols of life in

New York City. It challenges us to recognize the role that context plays in our perceptions of what is valuable and the importance of experience over product.

Most important, Banksy uses social media and people's interactions with it to create a multidimensional performance art model that lifts art up off the canvas and plants it firmly in the realm of experience. Going to see a Banksy is more like a treasure hunt than a day at a museum. By moving art into a new context, Banksy has shown us that you can open up new wide and diverse markets, simply by shifting your locale from inside to outside.

Law of We-volution 7

SUSTAIN GROWTH BUT MAINTAIN SCALE

Honeybees have a fascinating system in place to proliferate their species while maintaining a manageable scale within the hive. When a hive gets too big, it will make a new queen. Then, they will starve the existing queen until she emerges from her wax-encrusted nest and leaves the hive with a swarm of bees in search of a new home. The rest of the hive remains behind to serve their new queen.

Scale is an important consideration in business today, and a question on many entrepreneurs' lips is how do you stay small when you become successful and start to grow big? We can all take a tip from the bees on this score; they have realized that the key to sustaining growth while maintaining scale is to branch out and create new colonies of innovation that connect back to the original business. Reinvent your industry, discover a new one, strike out in a new direction and establish an outpost in a related but self-contained sector, and create new hubs of revenue and activity that can stay small but continue to grow and expand, colony by colony.

DECONSTRUCTION ON A PLATTER: FERRAN ADRIÀ

Ferran Adrià, known globally as "the best chef in the world," clearly illustrates how a brand can grow while maintaining the virtues of small size through a clever reshaping of its business model.

Adrià, the owner and executive chef of the world-renowned restaurant El Bulli, closed the doors at the height of its success, opting instead to run the establishment as a creativity foundation and a DNA lab that examines food, cooking, and creation in an attempt to isolate the essence of what works best about the old to better innovate the new.

Adrià opens El Bulli for one day here and there in order to host a "Lunch of Knowledge," billed as an "unheard of experience for the senses," which is presented as part of his "auditing the creative process" series. The Lunch of Knowledge brings together eight diners, who are selected through a competition, to enjoy a lunch in which Adrià reveals his creative process through his food. The lunch has eight courses, some real, some virtual, presented in a variety of formats so that diners can enjoy the dishes on both a sensory and a conceptual level. The lunches are recorded and broadcast later as documentary shorts.

As you can see, by shifting his business model from a restaurant to a creative forum, Adrià's brand grew at the same time that his traditional restaurant got smaller. In this way, by changing his organizational structure, Adrià has been able to invite the world into his restaurant, and still remain extremely exclusive and dedicated to small-batch ingenuity and culinary innovation, which can happen only in a small-scale environment.

ADAPT TO THE LAWS OF CREATIVE EVOLUTION

Law of We-volution 8
VALUE YOUR YOUNG

From an evolutionary standpoint, success is defined by the prosperity of future generations. You are successful only if you produce a successful next generation. Honeybees certainly understand this on a genetic level and have organized their colonies not only to nurture their young but also to teach them how to nurture each other by constantly engaging them in the service of the generations that come before and after them. Honeybees are assigned tasks based on their age, and their responsibilities change as they grow older. It is as if there were a system in place so that bees could learn the business from the ground up, so that they could have an appreciation for what every member does in the hive.

In the marketplace and for business today, youth is more valuable than ever. Hierarchies and the pomp and circumstance that many corporate cultures were once built on are things of the past. Today, new skills imagined by a younger generation should be as valued as the ideas coming from the hallowed hall of the boardroom. Learning to incorporate the next generation into every aspect of your business from top to bottom is critical to long-term success, particularly in today's rapidly shifting and technology-fueled landscape. Value your young, and foster engagement with and between them.

GOOGLE: A BOTTOM UP APPROACH

It's no surprise that Google, a bastion of innovation on a multitude of fronts and an often-cited best place to work, has a variety of programs in place to ensure bottom-up innovation occurs even in an organization of its size. They provide a good road map for how you can start to involve your youth in every aspect of your business, by fostering co-creativity and transgenerational communication in your workplace.

- Google places cafés in all of their headquarters to bring together people throughout the firm to share about their work and their lives.

- Every Friday at Google, employees of every level have an opportunity to ask questions of the senior leadership about matters that are concerning them and hear directly what their leaders have to say on those subjects.

- Google has a program called GUTS, or the Google Universal Ticketing System, which encourages employees to write in with their suggestions or concerns. GUTS communications are regularly reviewed and responded to.

- Google Moderator, designed by Goggle's engineers, is a management tool that allows everyone in the company to vote for questions they would like to be addressed during tech talks or company-wide meetings. Through this system, people can discover existing ideas, questions, or suggestions; vote for ideas; or generate new ones. Moderator is one of Google's famous 20 percent projects, which allow engineers to spend 20 percent of their workweek on projects that interest them. In this way, Google is able to tap into the many talents of its employees by enabling them to pursue their passions.

- Google FixIts are twenty-four-hour marathon sessions where everyone in the company comes together to solve a specific problem using their collective expertise.

- Googlegeist solicits feedback on hundreds of issues and then enlists volunteer employee teams across the entire company to solve the most important ones.

CREATIVE EVOLUTION REMINDERS

- Place creativity at the center of all of your business planning.

- Learn how to tell your business story in a way that inspires and motivates others.

- Make your business a democracy.

- Recognize the importance of everyone in your company, regardless of their level.

- Give back.

- Keep your finger on the pulse of culture.

- Always be on the lookout for new markets and resources.

- Stay small but include all.

- Value and nurture your young.

3.

Become an Artist of Business

Business art is the step that comes after Art. I started as a commercial artist, and I want to finish as a business artist. After I did the thing called "art" or whatever it's called, I went into business art. I wanted to be an Art Businessman or a Business Artist. Being good in business is the most fascinating kind of art. During the hippie era people put down the idea of business—they'd say, "Money is bad," and "Working is bad," but making money is art and working is art and good business is the best art.

—Andy Warhol

A little known story about Andy Warhol's iconic Factory is that, like so many of his debuts, it didn't open with a bang but with a chuckle. The Factory became a sensation as a result of an after-party designed to rescue a less-than-stellar gallery opening that might have destroyed Warhol's career. Instead, that infamous after-party wound up catapulting the

Factory and the work it produced into the stratosphere because of Warhol's legendary ability to turn disaster into dollars through artistic disruption.

ASSEMBLY-LINE ART

Warhol's second solo show opened at the Stable Gallery on the Upper East Side of Manhattan on April 21, 1964. Warhol was showing his new wood sculptures, which looked just like ordinary packing crates for common household items like Brillo pads, Del Monte peach halves, and of course, Campbell's soup. The boxes were the first pieces of art created at Warhol's new studio, which he had named the Factory, because he was making art on an assembly line.

Warhol devised his conveyer belt system in order to create more art in less time by delegating steps in the artistic process, generating hundreds of pieces of art that the artist's hand had never touched, except to sign. This was a revolutionary concept and challenged the fundamental notions of what was art and what was commerce.

Factory is as good a name as any. A factory is where you build things. This is where I make or build my work. In my artwork, hand painting would take much too long and anyway that's not the age we live in. Mechanical means are today, and using them I can get more art to more people. Art should be for everyone.

BECOME AN ARTIST OF BUSINESS

Turning Scandal into a Platform
for Media Success

Warhol's mass-production model proved very efficient indeed, particularly as he was quite good at getting his friends to work the line for free in exchange for artwork. As a result, there were literally hundreds of boxes littering the floors, stacked against the walls, and piled into towers in every nook and cranny of the small Stable Gallery. The art was everywhere, in the middle of the floors, scattered throughout the hallways, in doorways—everywhere but on the gallery walls—forcing gallery-goers to carefully maneuver around them so as not to trip over the art or each other.

The venue looked more like a warehouse than a tony Upper East Side art gallery that night. The art too, far from imparting a feeling of elegance and rare value, was virtually indistinguishable from the ordinary Brillo and Campbell's boxes that one might see in a grocery store. The art world was outraged, feeling that it had been made the butt of a bad joke. Warhol was accused of being a sellout, a capitulator to consumerism, a ruthless, money-hungry opportunist, and a fraud. The abstract expressionists in particular, the grand masters of their day, were livid. According to Gary Indiana, de Kooning screamed in Warhol's face "You destroyed art!"

Fortunately, the night wasn't over yet. Warhol's patron, Ethel Scull, a newly rich socialite who collected only pop artists just emerging onto the scene; the venerable Stable Gallery's owner Eleanor Ward, who specialized in high fashion and abstract expressionism; and Warhol himself, who mixed socially with the pop culture stars of the street, had planned an after-party to officially open the Factory.

Their combined guest lists—which included luminaries from high art and pop art, high fashion and hippie street style, high society and fringe society—made for a gathering so epic people have not stopped talking about it to this day. This signature, history-making mash-up of art with culture and culture with commerce established the Factory as the social and artistic hub of a generation. It made sensationalism the new advertising and made Warhol one of the most written- and talked-about artists of his or any day and, therefore, one of the most commercially successful artists in history.

From that point forward, even his detractors only added to the force of his impact. The more the art world railed about him, the more popular and famous he became. Warhol's after-party catapulted him and his Factory into the global spotlight, making his brand among the most popular, recognizable, and profitable in the art world.

The Warhol Economy

By 1970, Warhol was shattering records with the prices he commanded at auction. One of his soup cans sold for $60,000—mind-boggling for the time. By 2006, a painting from the Campbell's Soup Cans series sold for $11,776,000, which broke another world record. By 2013, Warhols were fetching prices in excess of $100 million.

BECOME AN ARTIST OF BUSINESS

In 2010, Warhol's work sold for a total of $313 million and accounted for 17 percent of all contemporary auction sales. This was a 229 percent increase over the previous year, proving that nothing could bounce back from a recession quite like a Warhol. He truly was the great rainmaker.

The media controversy that Warhol used as the platform for his business model persists today. Warhol's detractors still contend that his art was affectless and vacant and that the artist himself was morally bankrupt. Others contend that after Warhol was shot in 1968, he created no art of any significance and merely sought out rich and influential patrons like Liza Minnelli and Mick Jagger to feed his insatiable appetite for profit. His supporters insist that he did not stop creating relevant art after 1968 but merely switched out his canvas, morphing from a commercial artist into an artist of business, as Warhol himself said that he would.

Warhol did much more than create an artistic style; he created a business model and, moreover, a new way of living. While his revolutionary approach to mass-producing art through assembly-line silk-screening seems simple in light of today's technology, it was sufficient to teach the social media generation that anybody not only can be famous for fifteen minutes but can also become an artist in half an hour. Warhol showed us that we are all creative, and that people can and should use their lives and their businesses as canvases of co-creation and become artists of business.

Warhol's artistic philosophies and methods are now being

recognized as economic manifestos that are perhaps even more relevant for us today than they were for his generation. Now instead of being regarded as an eccentric who proposed a new way of looking at culture and gave birth to new art and artists, he has become the father of the equation that determines success in today's post-crash global economy of sharing: art + commerce + innovation.

THE WARHOL WAY

Artists such as Keith Haring (whose Pop Shop prefigured the pop-up shops we see fueling the marketplace today) and Robert Indiana (who successfully commodified the word *love*) flashioned themselves as businesses and thrived in the Warhol era, ushering in a widespread acceptance of pop art. Today's business leaders adapt those methods, positioning themselves as artists to infuse their brands with beauty and creativity.

Since nobody knew how to mix art with commerce better than Andy Warhol did, here are his rules, straight from his own mouth, about how to become an artist of business.

Good Business Is the Best Art

> *Being good in business is the most fascinating kind of art. Making money is art and working is art and good business is the best art.*

BECOME AN ARTIST OF BUSINESS

Recognizing that business is an art form and that you, as a businessperson, are an artist is critical to surviving and thriving in the sharing economy. Leading brands must see themselves as artists of business first and agents of commerce second.

Art today is the ultimate vehicle for transforming a common commodity into a sought-after treasure. Why? Because art transforms something that was once utilitarian into a vessel of engagement, as Warhol did with the Campbell's soup can.

Being an artist of business involves taking a product and turning it into an experience that engages the consumer and makes them a fan and loyalist for life because they are drawn both to the product and to the emotions the product evokes. Try thinking about your products and services from an artistic point of view. What feelings do you want to evoke in your customers? What feelings do you not want to illicit? Understand the creative and emotional impact of everything you do when it comes to your brand and learn how to create experiences, messages, stories, and systems that express the essence of that artistic vision.

HOW PEPSICO TURNED A BAG OF CHIPS INTO A WORK OF ART

PepsiCo demonstrated Warhol-inspired artistry with their Do Us a Flavor campaign, which invited customers to submit their ideas for new potato chip flavors. The campaign is a great example of business art that turned their product, a bag of potato chips, into a canvas for creative self-expression. This disruptive collaboration put potato chips front and center on the global stage by engaging the world in a co-creative conversation around a new generation of snack food, as imagined by the public and Pepsi.

As the contest was international, an amazing array of exotic and unusual flavor combinations—from chicken and waffle to onion Lakshmi to Fluffernutter to pumpkin blood—were submitted to a panel of judges, who chose finalists from each country and ultimately a winner. The winner received $1 million and got their picture on their bag of chips.

The Do Us a Flavor campaign generated over 3.8 million submissions, and sales of the original chips, as well as of finalist chips, went through the roof. The project also provided a ready and ever-renewing source of engaging content for the company's website and YouTube channels.

The Do Us a Flavor campaign illustrates that today, people don't just want to consume a product; they want to participate in the artistic endeavors brands can provide. And perhaps more important, this campaign demonstrates that creative experiences are what will influence purchasing decisions going forward, just as much as the quality of the product itself.

Change It Yourself

They always say time changes things, but you actually have to change them yourself.

Warhol's disruptive approach was intentionally designed to change the way we see, experience, and purchase art. Similarly, in business today, where technology has accelerated the pace of economic and social change, the ability to artistically disrupt yourself and your brand is critical.

In the modern market you have to take creative risks, challenge the status quo, turn a deaf ear to detractors, and push for changes that will make the world a more beautiful place. When you are constantly exploring avenues for seeing and experiencing life via your product, you are creating a studio environment that will produce the innovations that will engine your business in the future.

Today the Campbell's soup can piece is a masterpiece valued in the tens of millions. When it was first painted, however, it was regarded as an insult to art, and Warhol was viewed as a fraud. Warhol, confident in his ability to change things for the better, persevered with his vision because he knew that he was giving us something that we just didn't know we wanted yet. But he also knew that one day, we would want it a lot and pay plenty for it.

THE K-SWISS RETURN

There is perhaps no better modern-day demonstration of the Warhol notion of change then the recent return of K-Swiss.

Everyone in the over-thirty-five sneaker junkie crowd no doubt remembers the classic white-on-white silver-hooked beauties of the late 1980s and 1990s. Just looking at a white knight like K-Swiss brings a "say anything" smile to mind and puts a little bit of Wham! go-go back in your step.

Regardless of its former grooviness, the brand was virtually nonexistent during the beginning of the sneaker-head revolution that grew to spawn a litany of apps like Goodstuff and J23, designed simply to celebrate the love of, yup, you guessed it, sneakers.

K-Swiss knew that the passage of time would not bring their iconic footwear back in vogue, but that if they could turn back the clock and recapture the brand's old glory days by enabling their consumers to help them write the next chapter of their story, they just might be able to make what was old new again, in grand Warhol style.

Taking the Stan Smith–Pharrell Williams celebrity partnership idea designed to usher in a new generation of fans a step further, the K-Swiss campaign paired up with mega star Diplo to go beyond crowdsourced funding to the concept of collaborative co-created marketing.

In the sharing economy, a brand's ability to procure immersive experiences that stoke passions and emotional responses is as important as the products and services they purvey.

In the new groundbreaking campaign, K-Swiss allows people to apply for a position on the Board, a group of one hundred creatives, led by Diplo, whose ideas for brand outreach and growth will actually be implemented to put the legacy sneaker icon back on the map.

BECOME AN ARTIST OF BUSINESS

K-Swiss states that they are "committed to outfitting and inspiring a new generation of entrepreneurs" via their new campaign, with the same product, only presented in a new context.

In April 2015, the heritage tennis brand announced an impressive curriculum designed to educate members of the Board on the footwear and fashion industries with the intent of improving the K-Swiss brand.

The courses include Brand Positioning, taught by streetwear brand 10.Deep founder and designer Scott Sasso; Ideas with a Conscience, led by Tyler Gage and Dan MacCombie, co-founders of the Fair Trade–certified beverage company Runa; Sneaker Design, taught by Staple Design's founder and creative director, Jeff Ng; Lookbook Concept, led by Style .com fashion market director Rachael Wang; Social Media Best Practices, instructed by social media personality Josh Ostrovsky; and Writing Your Business Plan, taught by Sharmadean Reid, brand consultant and founder of London-based nail company WAH Nails. Quite an inspiring lineup.

Through the curriculum, members will learn how to write a new tagline for K-Swiss, create a lookbook, build a brand with a socially responsible mission, design shoes, cultivate a social media voice, and learn about the components of a business plan. The result is a revolutionized brand that is back in step with the leaders in its industry.

WE-COMMERCE

Interact and Connect

> *Human beings are born solitary, but everywhere they are in chains—daisy chains—of interactivity.*

Warhol lived and worked in constant connection with others. The Factory was designed to be an environment that had all manner of people constantly interacting in new and unusual ways. This was the inspiration for Warhol's art, and one of the reasons that he became more than a painter and grew into the founder of a movement that still has relevance today. In many ways, Warhol and his business model presaged the era of interconnected technology that we live in today, so modern-day artists of business can learn a lot from Warhol's approach to sharing.

The number one priority for contemporary brands should be to create for the we and not for the me. While that is counterintuitive to traditional business strategy, as consumption is an individual activity, brands that embrace we-ness and build community are the ones that will ultimately win at the increasingly competitive global game of instigating consumer participation.

WHY WEWORK WORKS SO WELL

WeWork is a contemporary embodiment of the principles that drove Warhol's Factory. It bills itself as a community of creators, and has created work spaces nationwide designed to house the entrepreneurs, small business owners, and artists of tomorrow, wherever they might live and work. WeWork is a business studio environment that appeals to innovators, mavericks, and artists who have left the constraints of corporate America behind and set off in pursuit of their own business missions with an eye toward building a better future.

Beyond office space, WeWork offers collaborative environments where trailblazers of all varieties can connect and share, resulting in countless mini incubators of business artistry. WeWork offers a panoply of services designed to instill and instigate creativity within its community. Amenities range from physical offerings like shared office space and conference rooms to networking opportunities and creativity festivals such as sleep-away camp retreats intended to facilitate collaborative imagination and productivity.

Famous for Fifteen Minutes

In the future, everyone will be world-famous for 15 minutes.

As Warhol predicted, in today's We-Commerce world, everyone is a brand, everyone has a voice, and everyone has access to a following that in some cases is extraordinarily large. In light of this, business artists must recognize that consumers have transformed from mere users of product to co-creators of content. Successful brands will tap into this collective urge to co-create with the products we consume and engage the stars in their community in a way that will halo back to the brand and create lifelong connections.

Brands of all kinds have to attract and grow a social media following across all currently relevant platforms in order to compete. More and more, follows and likes are the measure of success and brand loyalty, and it's incumbent upon you, as a business owner or marketer, to create content that engages your communities on a regular basis and adds value to your consumer's life. The days of the standard advertisement are quickly coming to an end. Brands must now become artists, creating arresting and immersive canvases that draw their consumers back again and again to delight and engage with their messaging. Just as Warhol predicted, not just people but brands must now achieve celebrity in order to compete. So think about what will make your brand famous within the context of social media and start a conversation with your community that will grow and expand commensurately with your business.

LIGHTS, CAMERA, SNACKTION!

The Doritos blockbuster Super Bowl tradition, Crash the Super Bowl, is an online contest that invites amateur filmmakers to submit their homemade Doritos ads for the chance to have their video broadcast during the game, before a Super Bowl audience of a hundred million viewers. Two winning ads are also presented globally on the Doritos website, and the creator of the ad that gets the most votes gets a check for $1 million and a life-changing opportunity to work for a full year onsite as a contractor at Universal Pictures.

Since its inception in 2006, Crash the Super Bowl has become a business art phenomenon and is now the largest online competition in the world. The user-generated ads are always a big hit, clearly demonstrating the power of engaging the creativity of your consumers through artful collaboration.

Contests are an excellent way to engage your consumers' creativity and get them invested in what your brand is doing. Figure out ways to engage your consumers or constituents in both the conversation around your marketing and in the creation of new offerings.

Find Meaning in Repetition

I'm afraid that if you look at a thing long enough, it loses all of its meaning.

Repetition was at the heart of Warhol's work, with images repeating in succession as if on filmstrips or newsreels. He played with repetition as a canvas in and of itself, because he understood the power that repetition has to both emphasize a point and, ultimately, distance us from what we are seeing. Warhol used repetition to demonstrate but also counteract the numbing effect of the repeated supersaturation of imagery in contemporary life, by pointing out the unique poetry of the images themselves.

Warhol was a master at duplicating objects in a way that causes us to see them in a fresh way each time we look at them. Further, he was famous for repurposing and reinventing his own work. Twenty years after he introduced the soup cans, he reused the idea, presenting them as minimalist, in black and white, changed to reflect a different time and culture, but using the very same image.

Today, just as Warhol foresaw, we are awash in repetitious imagery that comes at us from all directions day and night, with limitless competition and where big and small are on a level playing field. In a climate like this, the challenge for business artists is to find ever-changing and surprising ways to break through the complacency and boredom of repetition and touch people personally, every time you engage. Try to see your offering through multiple lenses and keep people guessing. How can you repurpose or reimagine what you have to offer the public to surprise and delight your consumers? How can you make something that was old and tired, new and fresh again by setting it in a new context? These are the kinds of questions you need to be asking yourself in order to stay relevant in a Warhol-inspired marketplace.

OREOS A LA CARTE

Food and beverage conglomerate Mondelēz's Oreo Snack Hacks campaign continues to fuel increased levels of consumption of a cookie that has been around for a hundred years and has become a commonplace product for most people. Recently, Oreo launched a web series showcasing top chefs "hacking" the sweet treat through the innovative use of Oreos in a variety of dishes.

This is just Mondelēz's most recent take on the Snack Hacks, which encourage their community to find new uses for the product and share them on video. A viral vine series was born that is inspiring Oreo lovers by the millions to reinvent the cookie. The Snack Hacks movement demonstrates for us all that if a business artist looks at something with fresh eyes and invites the participation of the consumer, it is likely that pathways to change will be illuminated, making an old product new and relevant again.

Become a Media Maker

When I got my first television set, I stopped caring so much about having close relationships.

Warhol called it way back when. Video is *the* most effective way to connect with other people. This is why he ultimately moved into the medium, which resulted in some of his most groundbreaking and lasting works of art. Warhol basically invented reality TV and Twitter, decades before anybody had even dreamed of a Real Housewife of New York

City, or an iPhone. And he designed his business model to capitalize on this understanding and made his art studio into a media studio.

Successful business artists today understand that companies have to evolve from providers of product into producers of content.

Entertainment and engagement are two of the most vital sources of innovation and brand longevity. With YouTube exploding as a $48 billion industry in its own right, the opportunity has arrived for brands to become the Factory studios of tomorrow. This changes the paradigm of communications from push to pull and puts the power of storytelling directly in the hands of the brand.

Just as Disney first delighted us with the majesty of the story of *The Lion King* and then sold us billions of dollars of related product, brands can and will do the same thing in the new era of sharing and engagement. Brands are the new studios. Think in terms of creating and delivering to your community entertainment vehicles that will not only facilitate engagement but move ancillary products that add value to the lives of your consumers.

THE NEWS FACTORY

In early 2008, after traveling to Singapore for the first time, I was awestruck by the progress I witnessed there. Everything was different. Citizen journalism was on the rise, and everyone had a voice. Technology-driven media outlets popped up daily, providing news in the blink of an eye as opposed to the course of a day, and traditional media publications looked less certain than ever—at a time when we had perhaps never needed them more.

Just when the world was at its most vulnerable, journalism, a bedrock of society in its role to serve and protect, was threatened by an overwhelming deluge of information intended more to entertain than to inform. It was becoming apparent that public relations centered on trying to maintain a dialogue with traditional media outlets were futile. Traditional news was drowning in the tsunami of information from new generation media sources too numerous to target or even count.

So what to do? Find a new profession? Inspired by Andy Warhol's communication strategies, I decided to cultivate my own version of Warhol's superstars and began establishing deep relationships with the growing pool of online journalists who increasingly dominated the shrinking traditional media landscape.

As outlets multiplied in number, they became less valuable than the specific personalities running them. I realized that traditional media would be able to stay afloat based on the celebrity of their journalists. In my mind, the dawn of an age of media superadvocates was born. No longer would you need to figure out how to pitch CNBC, *USA Today*, *Business Week*, and *Readers Digest* about your client/product/service. What you had to do instead was establish a relationship with just one of the top advocates of the day—for example, Maria Bartiromo, who had a show or column in every one of those outlets for an extended period of time in the first decade of the 2000s.

The topography was contracting, presided over by a growing pool of increasingly elite rulers. This meant that there would be a huge demand for the creation of content that truly informed and meaningfully engaged its viewers, and that role would be played by brands—not media outlets or journalists of any kind, as they would become too commoditized to be taken seriously.

In a business environment that increasingly rewarded purpose over standalone profit and stories over substance, I realized that brands would be tomorrow's studios. If you were brave and wise enough to be among the few who understood that, everything else above would just come along with it. This realization is what led me to create my own production company and YouTube channel, devoted specifically to these kinds of purposeful, story-driven examples of citizen journalism.

Reality

Land really is the best art.

One of the major themes in Warhol's work is that an artist can never compete with the beauty that reality can provide. This is why he painted ordinary objects, moments in reality, reproduced on a canvas to remind us of the power of experience.

We see the wisdom of this experience-driven business artistry today, with companies finding increasing popular success bridging the physical and digital worlds through events and experiences centered on art.

LEGOS AND GOOGLE: BRIDGING THE DIGITAL AND PHYSICAL WORLDS

Lego's newest product, Lego Fusion, has reinvented the concept of land by offering a multifaceted play experience in an entirely simulated landscape. Using physical bricks, children can build cars, castles, and more modest buildings, and then, through an app, they can upload their creations and interact with other builders, creating their own landscapes and designs, truly transforming a building experience into a shared artistic adventure. With this effortless exchange between the physical and digital realms, Lego is facilitating the merging of these two domains and driving intense engagement with its products in both.

Lego's example can help all of us to understand how to bridge the physical and digital landscapes. They show us how to merge material and virtual experiences in new and surprising ways that are designed to bring people together through a shared passion for art.

WE-COMMERCE

Die with Your Blue Jeans On

I want to die with my blue jeans on.

In his famous blue jeans quote, Warhol reminds us that brands are nothing if they don't provide moments that stir emotion and establish an unbreakable connection. Brands that are ubiquitous and have been around for decades have an advantage here, but even entirely new products can make the most of emotional connections, crafting a narrative and reaching a must-have status because they are able to define and represent a feeling for their customers.

Ask yourself what your brand means to you and to your customers emotionally. What draws them to the product or service, and how can you evoke an emotion that makes you an iconic best-in-class brand? What are the indelible moments that your offering can evoke for people that can be achieved by no other? Ask yourself these questions, and then broadcast the answers across all social media platforms to make your brand as unforgettable as Warhol's soup cans.

WHAT DO YOU DO IN YOUR LEVI'S?

Levi's are the denim version of Warhol's soup cans. Levi didn't just invent jeans as a must-have fashion item; they invented jeans as the first and only comfort fashion. Levi's are fashion's comfort food. We choose Levi's, not so much because of the jeans themselves but because of the iconic feeling they engender, feeling that the brand has gone to great pains to instill, playing on its legacy of going forth and exploring uncharted territories in a pair of Levi's jeans. Brands today need to artistically engineer iconic emotional associations that stem from the product because the product alone is no longer sufficient.

COME HOME TO STARBUCKS

Starbucks reenvisioned what getting a cup of coffee could be. Their stores are designed to encourage customers to linger, with comfortable chairs, plenty of tables, Wi-Fi, and relaxing music. People go to Starbucks as much for the comfort and sense of coming home that the stores provide as for the coffee. The company is currently in the process of connecting emotionally in a new way with their customer base, by partnering with Uber to provide the first one-stop order, pay, and deliver service for coffee.

ARTIST OF BUSINESS REMINDERS

- Art is no longer a luxury but a business currency.

- Harness change before it harnesses you.

- We are all interconnected, and there is no division between the personal and the professional.

- Brands are the new celebrities.

- Video is the most effective way to connect with your consumers.

- Ecosystems are the new business landscape.

- Mashing up elements that don't generally go together paves the way to innovation.

- Emotion and experience are creating today's iconic brands.

4.

Start Your Own Small-Town Silicon

America's industrial heartland, once a world-renowned beacon of American ingenuity and productivity, is now crumbling into extinction, causing many of us to question what that once proud union label "Made in the USA" means anymore.

With manufacturing jobs being outsourced overseas, auto plants laying off workers by the tens of thousands in towns all across the Rust Belt, and steel mills closing down, it's hard to imagine what will become of the original American Dream of making something out of nothing with your own two hands and finding health, wealth, and happiness as a result.

In places like Flint Michigan; Youngstown, Ohio; and Pittsburgh Pennsylvania, where the manufacturing plants have packed up and moved away leaving a swath of devastation and urban blight in their wakes, it's hard to imagine the next innovation that will turn Made in the USA back into a symbol for quality, ingenuity, and affluence.

But there is good news. America is again finding its place on the world stage through a renewed focus on passion and collaboration, creativity, and reinvention. The original ideas that fueled the nation way back when it was an emerging power, the ideas that made small the new big for the first time, are making a comeback and offer us important lessons about how to reinvigorate our communities and therefore stimulate business growth.

THE RUST FRONTIER: BRADDOCK GOES FORTH

There is perhaps no better example of the renewed spirit of America in motion than the story of Braddock, Pennsylvania, the town that Levi made famous in a series of documentary style ads with narratives like this:

> We were taught how the pioneers went into the west.
>
> They opened their eyes and made up what things could be.
>
> A long time ago, things got broken here.
>
> People got sad and left.
>
> Maybe the world breaks on purpose so we have work to do.

START YOUR OWN SMALL-TOWN SILICON

People think there aren't frontiers anymore.

They can't see how frontiers are all around
us . . . Go forth!

Braddock, Pennsylvania, is a prototypical American steel
town. It was once a thriving metropolis, a bustling, robust
economy fueled largely by the Edgar Thomson Steel Works,
which was Andrew Carnegie's very first steel plant, and
opened in 1873. Edgar Thomson was a gigantic facility, and
the very first steel mill to employ the latest innovation in steel,
called Bessemer technology. It allowed the production of steel
that was pure and therefore strong enough to allow for the
construction of skyscrapers.

In 1949, Braddock, whose entire city limits encompassed
only two-thirds of a square mile, was home to no less than
thirty tailors, fourteen jewelers, five banks, thirty-six real
estate agents, fifty-three restaurants, nine department stores,
fifty-one barbers, three newspapers, fourteen furniture stores,
and five car dealerships. Braddock's town slogan at that time
was "If you can't get it in Braddock, you don't need it." It was,
as its current mayor, John Fetterman, fondly recollects in his
TED talk, "the prototypical walkable community, before we
knew how awesome they were."

In the 1970s, the golden age of steel that was the envy
of the world came to a sudden and catastrophic end as a
result of, among other factors, the influx of imported and
less expensive steel, which the domestic manufacturers had

not prepared themselves to compete with. For Braddock, as for many steel towns in the Ohio Valley and across America, the fall from grace was sudden and almost impossible to recover from.

From 1970 to 1990, Braddock's population shrank from twenty thousand to just forty-six hundred, and by 2006 had dwindled to a mere twenty-three hundred residents, most of them African American single mothers living in poverty. The median income in Braddock was $17,000 a year for a family of four, and the average cost of a house was about $4,800. Many people were simply handing over their deeds for a dollar, just to get out of town. In just two decades, Braddock lost 90 percent of everything.

Reinventing Made in the USA

> *I dig this town's malignant beauty, its people and its history.*
> *To me, this is a place that should be saved.*
> —Braddock Mayor John Fetterman

John Fetterman first arrived in Braddock in 2001. After graduating from Harvard's Kennedy School of Government with a degree in education and social policy, he was hired to start a program for at-risk youth in Braddock. Fetterman, a six-foot, eight-inch hulk of a man with a shaved head and a tattoo of the Braddock zip code on his forearm, seemed perfectly suited to this crumbling scrap of the rust belt, despite his Harvard fine edges. Two years later, he bought a church, planning to convert it into a community center.

Next Fetterman bought the warehouse next door to live in while he converted the church, and four years later he ran for mayor, and won. Mayor Fetterman's first official act was to change the town's slogan to "Reinvention is the only option."

While Fetterman will be the first to tell you that his agenda is not a magic bullet and there are still many challenges to face in Braddock, there has been significant and instructive progress in the town. Braddock is no longer just another casualty of industrial blight but a new prototype for urban pioneering. It is a nationally recognized poster town for a new brand of community renewal enabled by technology and guided by the spirit of Silicon Valley. And that will make a difference not only for Braddock but also for lots of small towns with similar stories in America and around the world.

In eight years, Fetterman and his Braddock Redux foundation have restored a church and turned it into a community center, started a youth project that hires a hundred kids every summer to help rebuild the town, and created a two-acre farm where the condemned Main Street Hotel once stood. They raise communal crops in the shadow of the shuttered steel mill.

In a town with no playground, Mayor Fetterman built a

play village in the rubble of the old JCPenney. When the warehouses of the old Edgar Thomson plant had to come down, he harvested the colonies of honeybees that lived there and constructed a small-scale apiary to pollinate the farm. Beekeeping is now a popular elective at the Braddock Middle School.

Realizing that Braddock was a "food desert" where ice cream trucks were too faint of heart to venture, he opened the Community Café. Today, the Youth Project serves lattes and wraps in a café setting to a town that has no restaurant. Fetterman even funds an ice cream truck out of his own money to deliver free treats to the kids every two weeks.

In Braddock, they are creating housing for the homeless out of abandoned homes, attracting hip urban homesteaders with those $5,000 houses, and luring area artists with cooperative gallery and studio space. They are using art to combat the dark side of capitalism, and it is making a difference, one stained-glass window at a time.

Small-Town Social

Fetterman is doing something else too, which has, in a way, made all of this progress possible. He is making good use of social media, technology, and storytelling to get the global House of We involved with the fate of his community. Fetterman has made Braddock everybody's hometown that's fallen on hard times and has spread the story far and wide in a way that people care about. As a result, he has attracted deep-pocketed sponsors and investors, who have helped to make Mayor John and Braddock go viral.

After the Levi's campaign, which was filmed in the town and used actual Braddock residents as models (and paid them scale), Braddock became a part of Levi's brand republic. Levi donated over $1 million to pay for the conversion of Fetterman's church and continues to be involved in the town to this day. Recently, a major Hollywood movie filmed in Braddock, and Pearl Jam taped the sound track on Main Street.

This is why what is happening in Braddock is much larger than a "small town mayor makes good" story. What Fetterman has done has reimagined traditional American values through the lens of technology, just as Silicon Valley did years ago. He has put a new version of good old-fashioned American ingenuity, creativity, community, and hometown team spirit back to work in a fresh way. Like Silicon Valley, Braddock lights a path forward toward the next golden age for American industries and the American small towns that rely on them.

In the age of We-Commerce, collaboration and co-creation are fueled by an ability to connect but also by the realization of the power of a democratized global imagination. Today whether you are in the United States or Egypt, you have an equal chance of being heard.

THE SILICON SAGA

It all began with the transformation of an arid stretch of land in San Francisco now widely hailed as the global mecca of technological discovery. Silicon Valley. The name alone conjures visions of revolutionary gadgetry and goodness that will lead to prosperity and ideas that blend humanity with technology in order to imagine a better tomorrow.

While innovation today is at work doing all it can to bring traditional manufacturing sectors like autos and computers back to the United States with new tax incentives and energy benefits, our great nation is also embracing the idea of small as the new big, and allowing entrepreneurialism to organically take hold in small towns never before considered to be centers of production.

SILICON SUCCESS STORIES

Here are some of the more notable new American "Silicons" that are building new centers of ingenuity in their small towns through the use of art, culture, technology, and connection to community. Each one of these enclaves of innovation offers specific lessons about how to revitalize your brand community through creative We-Commerce, technological novelty, and community participation.

START YOUR OWN SMALL-TOWN SILICON

Silicon Forest

**KEY LEARNING: USE WHAT YOU HAVE TO
ATTRACT WHAT YOU NEED**

Located in the Portland, Oregon, metropolitan area, Silicon Forest began as an enclave of tech companies, predominantly computer hardware manufacturers, who had migrated out of Silicon Valley after the dot.com bubble burst. Silicon Forest is home to such tech industry leaders as Tektronix, InFocus, Planar, Pixelworks, Hewlett-Packard, and Xerox. But like the steel mills before them, manufacturing hardware hit a wall when confronted with cheaper foreign imports, and Portland had to reinvent itself and diversify.

One thing that the industrial district of Portland has in spades is abandoned buildings, which also means they have lots of cheap studio space to offer to a creative class. So the Portland Development Commission came up with the idea of a challenge to attract new types of businesses to Produce Row, in Portland's Eastside Industrial District. This is the Manifesto of Produce Row, which is both a brand and a coalition of businesses, and is attracting urban pioneers and tech settlers to reinvigorate and figuratively replant the forest:

> *HERE* is a special kind of here. Here is not a place for beige walls, suburban office parks and steady diets of sameness.
>
> *HERE*, the only place we use cookie cutters is in our restaurant kitchens. In this place we embrace

dichotomies and contradictions. Like trains sharing the road with bikes and tractor trucks parked amidst electric cars. Or quirky, upstart companies surrounding historic landmark Portland businesses.

HERE disruption is a piece of the landscape. HERE creativity paves every street. Every day is different and exciting and full of opportunity and that's just part of why we love it here.

HERE is Produce Row. . . .

The Startup PDX:Challenge, a contest initiated by Produce Row, offered the winners nine hundred square feet of office space, free for a year, in a building long ago used to assemble cars, later occupied by a rug dealership, and then home to a campaign field office for Portland's mayor. They also offered donated furniture; a $10,000 stipend; and free legal, accounting, and human relations services.

In May 2014, the commission announced the six winners: CoPatient, Safi Water Works, Walker Tracker, OnTheGo Platforms, ClutchPlay Games, and Alum.ni.

Produce Row is using the resources it has readily at hand to secure the resources that they need, all through the creative use of technology. As a result, Portland has emerged as a home for today's up-and-coming creative entrepreneurs and artists. In fact, there is now a comic sketch show devoted to the city, called *Portlandia*, which celebrates the inhabitants' eccentricities while also using the city as an example of the changing paradigms driving American art and commerce.

Silicon Anchor

KEY LEARNING: ANTICIPATE CONSUMER NEEDS BY STAYING ORGANICALLY CONNECTED TO YOUR ENVIRONMENT

Located in the Norfolk/Virginia Beach area, Silicon Anchor is a new center for entrepreneurship, reinvention, and start-ups focused around technology that is related to the area's long history as a ship port. What's most intriguing about the Silicon Anchor business community is its ability to innovate in response to its environment. Known for the construction, marine, and transportation industries, the region is building a hub of localized modernization founded on determining what businesses want before they know they want it and creating around that.

HoistCam is a textbook example of the kind of work occurring in this region and what it can teach us. The brainchild of GM Engineering Services, HoistCam is a rapidly deployable wireless electronic night/day camera platform designed to serve the needs of crane operators across many industries. HoistCam eliminates blind spots by placing the eyes of the crane operator anywhere. Safety is increased and efficiency improved by making visual information instantly available.

WE-COMMERCE

Silicon Bayou

KEY LEARNING: EMPLOY DISRUPTION IN GOOD TIMES AS WELL AS IN BAD

Post-Katrina, and perhaps because of the catastrophic destruction that the 2005 hurricane brought with it, New Orleans has become a model of renewal. Starting with a blank canvas, New Orleans has reevaluated how to provide its citizens with fundamental services in a new and better way, because after Katrina, the old systems no longer functioned. Today, the city continues to expand on the insights gathered during hardship and is disrupting its way to a new boom economy. Following is a list of New Orleans companies that are not only helping redefine the region but also reconfiguring the spheres within which they do business:

- FundDat is a crowdfunding platform for projects created in or about New Orleans. The platform raised over $23,000 for local projects during their beta launch. As corporate leadership transitions from the few to the many, crowdsourcing continues to be a vital avenue for everything from idea development to funding. By taking a broad new business model and customizing it specifically to a region, FundDat exemplifies the "think global, but act local" philosophy that defines the new economy. Hyperlocal approaches to everything from product development to marketing will drive success in the new world order.

- mSchool is an innovative start-up that helps communities open and lead one-classroom micro-schools. In as little as two weeks, mSchool works with communities and schools to turn any space into a state-of-the-art learning lab where students can make multiple years of academic progress each year. This brand has taken key lessons from the regions which needed pop-up schools after Katrina to accommodate the children whose schools had been destroyed and applied this knowledge on an ongoing basis to all their projects, showing that disruption is equally important in times of prosperity as it is during days of destruction.

Silicon Beach

KEY LEARNING: HARNESS TECHNOLOGY TO TELL YOUR STORY FAR AND WIDE

Located in the greater Los Angeles metropolitan area, Silicon Beach is home to more than five hundred tech start-up companies. Major tech residents include Google, Yahoo, YouTube, AOL, EdgeCast Networks, and MySpace. Silicon Beach is also home to a number of start-up incubators such as Launchpad LA, Amplify.LA, and StartEngine, which are all accelerators for promising new ventures.

What the region has done best is to capitalize on two of the things that make Hollywood tick—video and celebrity—in order to create a new mecca of regional development.

WE-COMMERCE

Silicon Beach companies understood that one of the keys to a successful reinvention is to figure out how to link your hometown industry to the future of technology. Hollywood continues to be the entertainment capital of the world, and one of the fastest growing areas in technology is mobile entertainment. So Silicon Beach has harnessed this trend and made itself the place to be for collaborative entertainment fueled by technology.

Silicon Alley

KEY LEARNING: INVENT NEW MODELS TO REPLACE OBSOLETE SYSTEMS

Silicon Alley is a haven of tech innovation in Lower Manhattan, rising literally up out of the ashes of 9/11. The industries in the alley are largely centered on media and e-commerce, cranking out new white-hot tech companies and generating disruptive concepts.

Silicon Alley shows us that technology doesn't just remake traditional industries but imagines entirely new experiences. From BuzzFeed giving media a makeover to Birchbox mashing up the notions of social club and mail order service, the leading titans of the Alley understand that the key to success today is creating new collaborative experiences that can reshape the world in ways that are restorative and inventive.

START YOUR OWN SMALL-TOWN SILICON

Silicon Bridge
KEY LEARNING: BUILD IT AND THEY WILL COME

Silicon Bridge, located in Brooklyn's DUMBO section, is a residential enclave tucked between the waterfront and downtown Brooklyn. DUMBO is home to Etsy, an explosively successful online marketplace for crafters and artists of all kinds. It also is host to countless small marketing agencies, which over the past decade have made their headquarters in former factories with sweeping views of the Brooklyn Bridge, the Manhattan Bridge, and the Hudson River.

Today, the historic neighborhood is also touted by New York City as a start-up hub and the first Brooklyn appendage to Manhattan's Silicon Alley. According to NYC Digital, an initiative affiliated with the mayor's office, 139 small firms or start-ups call DUMBO home.

What's coolest about DUMBO is not one company in particular but the sense of community-wide focus on artistic progress. Whether it's DUMBO Startup Lab, the reconstruction of Empire Stores, which is being billed as New York's next big tech and business epicenter, or the Brooklyn Tech Triangle, the area has become a magnet for the world's pioneering, energetic, and creative entrepreneurs and has emerged as the city's largest cluster of tech activity outside of Manhattan. DUMBO is a textbook example of building a hub of regionalized innovation from the outside in, leading with superior infrastructure that daily reaffirms the old adage that if you build it, they will come.

Silicon Desert

**KEY LEARNING: WHEN THE RULES GET IN
YOUR WAY, CHANGE THEM**

Nevada is hard at work ensuring its future as a hub of entre-preneurial activity. Home of legendary Internet shoe titan Zappos, Nevada also just recently landed the fish among fish to base its HQ in the state: the luxury electric car manufac-turer Tesla will be moving to Nevada to open a plant, in a deal worth $1.25 billion.

The key reason they won the deal? Disruptive innova-tion fostered through tight collaboration between the public and private sectors. Nevada vowed to change legislation that prohibited Tesla from cutting out auto dealers and selling directly to the consumer. It was this flexibility and forward thinking that allowed Nevada to beat out Arizona and vari-ous other states to be home of the Tesla Gigafactory, clearly raising the bar for who deserves the Silicon Desert title.

The key to the future of collaborative innovation and invention is to involve the public sector closely in private sec-tor development. Tearing down the barriers of segregation between the public and private sectors will serve a dual pur-pose, helping to support the best ideas of tomorrow that will benefit society as well as to push for government practices that can actually work.

Silicon Harbor

**KEY LEARNING: CREATE A VIBRANT CULTURE THAT
ATTRACTS A CREATIVE CLASS**

Located in Charleston, South Carolina, Silicon Harbor is home to some of the largest and fastest growing companies in America. For example, BiblioLabs, makers of BiblioBoard, has created an unlimited multiuser platform that helps libraries affordably bridge the digital divide and support life-long learning for all members of the community, which is really taking hold globally

BiblioLabs was the first of three local tech companies within a three-mile radius to have been put on the Inc. 500 Fastest Growing Companies list in the last year. BiblioLabs ranks at number seven on Inc.'s media company list, just behind Facebook. Not bad for a start-up that began with four people working out of a small downtown apartment in 2006. The tech buzz, combined with a burgeoning music industry that has Charleston being hailed as the new Nashville, has attracted a creative class and top talent from around the world.

Young entrepreneurs and tech lovers are relocating to pursue their passions and find their ideal work–life balance. With a heavy emphasis on food, fashion, and a rich cultural history, Charleston provides a lifestyle that is enjoyable and rich in independent spirit.

Charleston has demonstrated that in the age of We-Commerce, success is supported by a proper work–life balance and accelerated by creativity and culture. As disruption continues to close the gap between culture and commerce, those communities and brands that can foster high levels of both will come out on top.

Pages from Billee's Playbook
BOSTON BOB DAVIS

In the late 1990s the first tech boom was under way and everyone was fighting to become the next "it" dot-com. In those days, success as an Internet company wasn't achieved by providing the best online experience, it was simply about what you could sell to consumers with the click of a mouse, in the privacy of their own homes or offices. The sheer novelty of e-commerce was enough.

At the time, I was a vice president at Shandwick in the days that predated the merger of Weber and Shandwick and then Weber Shandwick and BSMG, which made Shandwick, or Weber, the largest and most revered PR firm in the world.

The agency, like all the rest, was actively trying to court the Internet champions of tomorrow, and in that quest they were fortunate enough to win the Lycos account. Lycos was one of the top search engines and stood among the ranks of companies like AOL and Yahoo!. Lycos was based in Waltham, Massachusetts, and was run by notorious Dorchester bad boy and business genius Bob Davis.

Bob, unlike many of the silver-spooners who were running the other Internet powerhouses, had not come up in the

Ivy Leagues and the hallowed halls of Wall Street, but rather was a Boston boy through and through, with an accent thick enough to make a Kennedy blush. Davis had just taken Lycos public to soaring results, making it one of the fastest IPOs in history at the time. Following that milestone achievement, Davis and his team were looking for a PR partner to tell their story and showcase their unique attributes with an eye on gaining a foothold against mighty competition.

Fortunately for the agency, and for me, we were selected as the Lycos agency of record, responsible for everything from consumer and tech PR to financial and business media relations. In our years together at Lycos, Davis and team appeared in standalone profile stories in every media outlet from the *Wall Street Journal* to *BusinessWeek* to the *New York Times*, and the company was soon seen as a fierce competitor in the space, who while lagging behind the big boys in key consumer areas, ranked top of the heap when it came to financial performance and leadership.

Davis sold Lycos to Telefónica for an astounding $12.5 billion right before the market crash of the late 1990s. He walked away having built one of the greatest Internet companies on the planet and sold it for a whopping fee all in the span of a few years. Davis left to glowing headlines globally but faced questions at the time about why he had sold. Did he get out too quick? There was so much left to do.

In typical Bob Davis style, he wasn't gone for long, returning a year later, after the market had tanked, with an autobiography titled *Speed Is Life*, which talked of his days at Lycos and his departure (which clearly was the right move despite what any of the early skeptics had to say). Davis kept me around for years after his Lycos departure for projects here and there; whenever he could give me an opportunity he did. Many years later he hired my team when I was an executive vice president at Weber to help raise awareness about Highland Capital Partners, where Davis still is today. Highland Capitol Partners is a renowned organization responsible for supporting some great companies, such as Lululemon, Quigo, Quattro, and CafeMom. The firm is also a key contributor to the world's reverence toward Boston as a mighty competitor for Silicon Valley. Take a look, and you'll find that everyone from *Forbes* to the *Wall Street Journal* has covered this notion.

Through my years with Davis, I was privileged to watch Massachusetts rapidly become one of the most productive tech corridors in the world today. This is so self-evident that they don't need to be called Silicon Boston, because the notion of Silicon Valley's dominance comes into question as a result of only one player, and that is Boston and its surrounding areas.

As a result of a deep culture of entrepreneurialism and strong ties with institutions such as Harvard and MIT, Boston clearly demonstrates the power of building a unified local ecosystem that brings together technology, educational institutions, and the community in ways that make the new Made in the USA something that is already a legend as opposed to a new trend.

SMALL-TOWN SILICON REMINDERS

- Be resourceful and imagine new uses for resources you have in surplus.

- Establish an organic and lasting connection with your region and community.

- Disruption is not just a crisis response anymore.

- Learn to access technology to spread your message.

- Find new systems that make the obsolete relevant again.

- Pioneer new urban creative centers out of the rubble of the industrial past.

- Transform legislation to make the impossible possible.

- Build a business community that's fun to hang out in.

5.

Learn the New Geography
of Global Innovation

Over the last twenty years the world was forever altered by the advent of the Internet and its awesome power to make the universe truly connected as well as increasingly small. It's not only the global consumer demography that has been changed, but the topography and geography of global commerce. The world is once again flat, because technology has put everyone from Tel Aviv to Cupertino on an even playing field.

As the notion of entrepreneurialism and a middle-class sensibility goes global, the idea of a flat world does more than make the universe a smaller place. It makes unbridled innovation globally available, regardless of a country's size. This is taking shape everywhere you can imagine, not just in areas known for industrial advancement and technological discovery, but in remote and unlikely places that the average person would find difficult to locate on a map, let alone visit.

MADE IN THE X

The hyper-local "Made in X" movement is no longer specific to America but playing out on a world stage. This is happening for two reasons:

1. Technology has democratized innovation and creation, making it an accessible activity for anyone, anywhere.

2. The world's economic center of gravity is rapidly moving from west to east. Superpowers and emerging market economies once known as the unrivaled centers of excellence in new development are increasingly being challenged by "frontier" economic engines in places so far flung that they make Brazil and India seem tried, true, and familiar.

The superpower economies found in Europe, Asia, and America continue to thrive, commensurate with their appetite for reinvention and disruption, but are no longer untouchable in specific big industries nationally. America is no longer just known for manufacturing or automotive production in hubs such as Detroit and Chicago. Europe is no longer composed strictly of old-school economies like France, Germany, and England but is now buttressed by many rapidly developing regions in eastern Europe—Croatia and Romania, for instance. And Japan is but one of a multitude of Asian nations known for auto and consumer electronic invention.

It's interesting that the BRIC nations (Brazil, Russia, India, and China), once regarded as *the* places to look for emerging market practices, are slowly but surely becoming much more akin to superpower economies, with China now responsible for driving growth not only in Asia but in the entire world. The same is true for Brazil, Russia, and India. Today, São Paulo is more like Seattle than Sardinia.

THE NEXT FRONTIER

In place of the once-revered emerging market BRIC nations, new frontier economies located in Southeast Asia, the Middle East, and Africa are exploding onto the scene. On this nascent frontier of innovation, nations such as Singapore are becoming new hubs for global corporate headquarters. Tel Aviv has emerged as the closest rival to Silicon Valley, and Africa has given birth to seven different individual economies worth noting, within an ecosystem of twenty-plus engines of commerce that are all growing daily.

These are the economies that will be responsible for much of the future growth of multibillion-dollar conglomerates like Unilever and Pepsi. This is a direct result of the emerging global middle class that drives consumption but also is due to the hotbeds of ingenuity that are pumping life into this new frontier.

Silicon Valley and the ideas and values that drive it have gone global. These international pockets of innovation, some of which have their own Silicon-inspired monikers, offer invaluable lessons to all of us about how to succeed in business on a global scale.

Silicon Wadi, Tel Aviv, Israel

KEY LEARNING: MASH-UP TECHNOLOGICAL ADVANCEMENT WITH ENTREPRENEURIALISM TO CREATE A VITAL ECOSYSTEM OF GROWTH

With five thousand start-ups, the Silicon Wadi ("valley" in Arabic) of the Mediterranean closely shadows Silicon Valley as the number two place where innovation flourishes globally.

Tel Aviv has achieved its notoriety due to the highest density of start-ups in the world and has sixty-one companies listed on NASDAQ. From BillGuard's crowdsourced personal finance security to Wix.com's web publishing tool and Cardboard Technologies' biodegradable bicycle, the start-up landscape in Tel Aviv has a reputation for being the most inventive city in the world. It's no wonder Google invested in Tel Aviv offices.

There is no question that Tel Aviv tops the list for far-flung and newly imagined revolutionary invention. Why? The key components responsible for Israel's dominance are important to the development of any brand in the global we-conomy:

1. **Tech talent:** Fueled by the private sector and funded by governmental and public organizations, Tel Aviv has dedicated itself to targeting and fostering technological talent through a committed and consistent investment in education.

2. **Entrepreneurial talent:** Israel is flush with independent businesspeople, second in number only to Silicon Valley. Having an R&D center in Israel means Tel Aviv is able to tap into this stellar talent bank and fund it, creating a highly productive, innovative, and collaborative work environment that gets the job done.

3. **Ecosystem:** The long list of companies in Israel includes Intel, Google, SAP, HP, IBM, EMC, Apple, Huawei, Samsung, GE, Philips, Siemens, Alcatel-Lucent, Oracle, Microsoft, Motorola, Xerox, AT&T, Dell, AMD, PayPal, McAfee, Qualcomm, Polycom, Marvell, Cisco, Telefónica, Avaya, Deutsche Telekom, SanDisk, eBay, AOL, Autodesk, Yahoo!, Sears, GM, and LG. The number of businesses operating in the Silicon Wadi and the plethora of talent and ingenuity available there are motivating businesses to shift their R&D efforts to Israel, connecting Tel Aviv to a global development ecosystem.

Silicon Nicosia, Cyprus

KEY LEARNING: MAKE COLLABORATION A CORE BUSINESS COMPETENCY

The WIPO cites Cyprus as a country showing great potential in technological discovery, despite its recent financial crisis. Companies like NCR and TSYS have caught on, choosing the Mediterranean island capital for their regional headquarters. With its high per capita income, favorable tax system, sophisticated infrastructure, and low business set-up costs, the possibilities are prime in Cyprus. Bitcoin marketers Neo & Bee just opened in Nicosia, bringing the notion of virtual currency even further east.

Start-ups funded by creatively adaptive young entrepreneurs are flooding the landscape as Cyprus aims to rebuild itself as a world-class hub of economic disruption. NIPD Genetics, StudentLife, and AtYourService are just a few of the new companies with potential for enormous global expansion taking hold in this fertile region of opportunity.

The key learning to glean from Cyprus concerns the power of cooperation and the actualization of collaborative commerce. Cypriot companies are created by entrepreneurs exchanging ideas and working together to shape the future of the country. Startup Live, Startup Weekend, TEDxNicosia, Global Entrepreneurship Week, and Hack Cyprus are just a few of the festivals that occur each year in Cyprus, bringing the best minds in the world together to share ideas and grow.

The rapid developments in the Cypriot start-up ecosystem

have inevitably caught the eye of investors both in Cyprus and abroad, who see great opportunities for returns in some of these high-growth start-ups. The start-up revolution is unfolding fast and can undoubtedly play a significant part in the next economic miracle in Cyprus.

Silicon Vietnam

KEY LEARNING: BE BOLD AND AUDACIOUS

Following the lead of China, Japan, and the Asian tigers, Vietnam recently launched the ambitious Silicon Valley Project: a comprehensive plan to transform the country from a top producer of electronic components to a major player in the global digital economy. Sponsored by the Ministry of Science and Technology, the project aims to launch internationally competitive technology firms and eventually turn one of the country's major cities—Hanoi, Ho Chi Minh City, or Da Nang—into a tech hub.

Flappy Bird, the mobile game developed by Hanoi programmer Nguyen Ha Dong, illustrates the untapped potential of Vietnamese tech start-ups as well as the challenges they face. Dong's success emphasizes for all that in today's technologically flattened world, anyone, anywhere can innovate— no matter how simple the design or subtle the voice—if they are bold and audacious enough to make themselves heard.

Silicon Turkey

KEY LEARNING: DO ONE THING AND DO IT BETTER THAN ANYBODY ELSE

A huge factor in Turkey's start-up success is the country's demographics. The majority of the country's population is young and mobile-connected. This level of connection to fellow regional innovators and the wider world as a result of technology has ignited a new wave of development in the region. Innovation Silicon Turkey–style combines the best of the old craftsmanship and artistry that helped build the region historically with the benefits of the world's most inventive technologies.

Thanks in large part to social media, young Turks are finding inspiration and guidance from the start-up progress in other parts of the world. While Turkey's move toward a start-up ecosystem has been building for years, cutting-edge ideas around emerging technology—like wearables such as smart watches and mobile commerce systems that make purchasing through phones faster and easier—are set to outpace e-commerce in the next few years. Istanbul has even become an elite bellwether of the viability of future technologies. With such notable success, Turkey holds a place at the forefront of innovation.

The key learning to be gleaned from Turkey's expansion is its surgical focus on picking one thing—one new thing—and doing that one thing better than anyone else. As the rest of the world continues to celebrate the wonders of e-commerce,

WE-COMMERCE

Turkey understands that the future resides with purchases made over mobile phones rather than laptops and is championing an m-commerce revolution.

Here are a few examples:

- Trendyol—a Turkish version of Gilt—has demonstrated massive appeal, bringing products and purchasing power directly to mobile technology.

- Lidyana, a mobile fashion retailer backed by Endeavor, and Hepsiburada, an Amazon-like e-marketplace partnering with international software company ThoughtWorks, are working to bring much-needed mobile commerce potential directly to consumers.

- BiTaksi, a Flywheel- or Uber-like app, matches locals and especially tourists in Istanbul, Ankara, and Antalya with hard-to-find cabdrivers via mobile.

- Yemek Sepeti offers remote food ordering and delivery to smartphone users, almost like a Turkish GrubHub or Seamless.

Turkey has both invented and defined an entire category in which the most creatively disruptive ideation can and will originate. The private sector is leveraging mobile to address the country's unique demands and define a new m-commerce-driven economic ecosystem. We can all learn a great deal from the granularity and focus of Turkey's progress, enabled by their decision to do just one thing better than anybody else in the world and build their future on that one, finely honed skill.

Silicon Bandung
KEY LEARNING: BE START-UP FRIENDLY

It is no secret that Southeast Asia is among the most fertile grounds for innovation today, and Bandung is now giving Jakarta a run for its money as the development capital of Indonesia. With over 60 percent of the population under forty, the plentiful workforce is young and tech savvy. In addition, the pleasant climate and the country's focus on developing local cuisine combine to make Bandung a real contender. Just to give you an example, Bandung is Twitter's sixth biggest user base in the world.

Bandung Digital Valley (BDV) is a business incubator devoted exclusively to emerging technology companies— start-ups that produce everything from web applications to online services. BDV was founded in December 2011, and by 2012 it launched its first program, called Indigo Incubator. Indigo provides money and resources for start-ups, including technical, financial, and design support in addition to market access and a payment system for customers. In 2013, Indigo Incubator launched ten start-ups after putting them through a seven-month training program. Of those that have been launched, two are rising in prominence:

- **Jarvis Store** is an online shopping site that is specially designed to be compatible with various computing devices, from notebook computers to tablets and smartphones.

- **Cerita Perut**, building on the famous food of the region, is an online culinary community featuring recipes and restaurant reviews. The company was formed in 2009 and now has twenty-three thousand participants from across Indonesia as well as major sponsors.

What Silicon Bandung teaches us is that creating a start-up-friendly environment requires a combination of elements including youth, a vibrant culture, government support, a tech-savvy population, and great food! Globally, the new centers of tech innovation are proving that lifestyle and culture play a strategic role in business success.

Silicon Morocco

KEY LEARNING: INNOVATION MUST MOVE FROM TOP DOWN AND BOTTOM UP

The Morocco Innovation Initiative is an intersection of strategies designed to build a creative ecosystem with a horizontal structure that encourages ideas to flow from top to bottom and bottom to top. The initiative was developed through a participatory approach with representatives from a variety of major sectors: administrations, universities, research centers, enterprises, civil society, and finance. Gaps were identified along the innovation chain, and strategic action and policy plans were conceived in order to address them.

During the First Moroccan Innovation Summit, held in June 2009 to launch the initiative, nine agreements were signed among many players belonging to different institutions and ministries. These policies intend to meet the following challenges:

- Reinforcing Moroccan enterprises' competitiveness

- Making Morocco a producer of technology

- Exploiting Moroccan universities' R&D capacities

- Making Morocco attractive for R&D talents and projects

- Fostering a real culture of innovation and entrepreneurship

In the age of We-Commerce, the notion of collaboration and co-creation is supported by harnessing the power of a democratized global imagination. Today whether you are in the United States or Egypt, you have an equal chance of being heard and revered, and whoever wins does so based on the merit of his or her idea, not on the locale from which it was derived.

NEW GEOGRAPHY
OF INNOVATION REMINDERS

- Blend innovation with entrepreneurialism to create an ecosystem of growth.

- Collaboration is key.

- Set ambitious goals and go after them with gusto.

- Do just one thing, but do it better than anyone else.

- Invest in local culture to create a start-up friendly environment.

- Create a democracy of ideas.

6.

Homebrew Your Own Cult

How did a loosely organized and contrarian jug jam band in northern California who did everything they weren't supposed to do businesswise become one of the most successful and influential musical acts of all time? And how did a couple of adolescent techno-nerds tinkering with their toys in a garage in Menlo Park manage to transform the entire culture and reshape the global economy in just four short years?

The secret behind the rapid and breathtaking success of these two counterculture-driven brands is that they had glimpsed the powerful possibilities inherent in a we-conomy and designed their business models in harmony with these ideals. Instead of selling a product, the Grateful Dead and Apple were sharing their creativity in forums that unified people. By making this one central shift in thinking, each amassed a huge and passionately loyal community of the faithful who will follow them wherever they go.

THE RISE OF CULTING

In the past people were loyal to brands simply because of name recognition, status, or taste. Thanks in large part to the innovations of Apple, the Grateful Dead, and others we now demand as much from our brands as we used to expect from our churches. We expect to be inspired, enlightened, comforted, defined, and redeemed. We want to be engaged creatively, spiritually, socially, and emotionally.

We expect our brands to lead us to a better life, teach us a better morality, put us in touch with other souls just like us, and help us find ways to give something back to the world around us. And we expect our brands to give back too. This has given birth to an entirely different relationship between people and the products they buy and support, which looks and feels more like a faithful following than brand advocacy. Today, when people say they would rather fight than switch, they really mean it.

In this new "culting" environment, people connect with brands and create dialogues not only with them but also through them. Creatively destructed brands who are agile and able to respond to this impulse are consciously employing the same devices used by traditional cult leaders and faith-based organizations to create and grow living and breathing cults that invite us in to live, love, play, believe, evangelize, and worship.

Just as the House of Jobs and the House of the Dead did, brands now look to ignite passion, inspire belief in a particular ideology, encourage rivalry, and inspire loyalty. They provide strong and inspiring leadership, encourage total immersion in the cult experience enjoyed in communion with others, and place an emphasis on the power of we rather than me. Brands have transformed from merchants of goods into merchants of doing good, and cults are banding together behind a common brand ideal and taking it to the streets in a whole new way.

This central pivot has changed not only the way brands are marketed but the way audiences are aggregated and our economy is driven, transforming the world's number one currency from cash to socialization, creativity, and sharing. Culting has changed the role brands will play in society—going from mere purveyors of product to creators of the thoughts, ideas, content, attitudes, and collective movements that their members demand and will define tomorrow's shared reality.

WHAT THE GRATEFUL DEAD AND APPLE HAVE IN COMMON

The easiest way to think about brands like the Grateful Dead and Apple is to think of them as religions, or cults, because both brands function much like churches do. They are passion-driven institutions that inspire belief in a better world, share a strongly held code of ethics, a common goal that fosters a sense of community, and provide lots of built-in opportunities for engaging the faithful on a mass scale and converting them into evangelists for the brand's cause.

Grateful Dead fans don't just like to listen to Grateful Dead music, they worship in the church of the Dead. They buy every new product and share bootleg recordings and concert memorabilia. They religiously go on tour right along with the band members, following their musical gurus to each and every venue in search of those one-of-a kind experiences that can be enjoyed only together.

Apple fanboys behave in the very same way. They don't just prefer Apple products; they wait on line for hours in order to buy the newest and latest offering from the church of Apple. They worship the late Steve Jobs and weave heroic legends around Apple's leaders. They devour every revolutionary new accessory, application, or upgrade with religious enthusiasm and hang out together in genius cathedrals (otherwise known as Apple stores), just having fun plugging stuff in to see how it works. They share a common ideology, a disdain for the mainstream, an irreverence for authority, and a passion for design and artistry. They adore innovative technology that does really cool stuff just because it can, and they all despise Bill Gates.

This is not a brand following or even a fan base. This is a passionately devoted and religious following, the members of which will likely remain loyal for life. Although they are from different industries, producing different products for different reasons, Apple and the Grateful Dead have a lot in common, and this is not by accident. There is a science to culting, and we can learn much about how to accomplish it by looking at the founders of the modern brand cult.

TIPS FOR HOMEBREWING YOUR OWN CULT

Here is what we can learn from the founders of culting about how to harness the power of sharing by building a cult of your own.

Provide Opportunities

Provide opportunities for passionate engagement on a mass scale that will convert customers into evangelists who will spread the gospel and recruit new members.

THE CULT OF THE DEAD

The Grateful Dead did literally everything wrong according to the prevailing marketing wisdom of the day for how to make money in the music business. For the Dead—who started their career as the house band for Acid Test parties held by *One Flew over the Cuckoo's Nest* author Ken Kesey in San Francisco—it was always more about the concerts than the record sales. They were primarily a performance band, a happening, almost a transcendent experience.

WE-COMMERCE

Where most concerts were strategic, uniform, and disengaged, a Dead performance was organic, spontaneous, and intensely and passionately connected to the audience. The live experience was a unique product in and of itself, and as such turned the artistry and co-creativity of a rock concert into a commodity and a currency all its own.

This shift in thinking not only completely changed the quality and character of the attendees' experience but turned the way in which a musical brand went about achieving and sustaining success on its head. The Grateful Dead approached their brand as a we-based model centered on inclusivity, sharing, and a creativity-driven bottom line rather than the prevailing me-based model centered on exclusivity, use restriction, and bottom line–driven creativity.

For the Dead the only formula was jamming, having fun, and creating unique musical experiences that were best enjoyed collectively, where nothing ever happened the same way twice and where capitalism took a back seat to unbridled creative expression. This resulted in the development of a passionate group of fans, who follow the band wherever it goes, decades after the band was first formed. The evolution of a whole new generation of music experiences of mass scale inspire and attract enormous and faithful cult followings.

HOMEBREW YOUR OWN CULT

Belong to a Brand Family

Engineer a sense of belonging to a brand family that is united by a common purpose and led by a charismatic and visionary leader.

THE CULT OF APPLE

Steve Jobs was a child of the 1970s, and he worshiped in the church of the counterculture, just like the Dead did. He had the same passion for changing the world one performance at a time and the very same ability to create and sustain a faithful cult following through passionate engagement.

The difference is, where the Deadheads happened by accident, the cult of Apple was created on purpose. Jobs knew exactly what he was doing when he put the accidental genius of the Dead into intentional action. This is the reason Apple's first marketing director, Guy Kawasaki, who studied business by listening to televangelist Billy Graham, was called the Chief Evangelism Officer.

Jobs wanted to create a product that would give the power of information to the people. In creating Apple, and the cult of Apple, Jobs didn't just found a successful computer company, he gave the counterculture a way to change the world from the inside out. Once the counterculture and the revolutionary thinkers and creative explorers had to demonstrate in the streets and attack mainstream society from the outside in. Now, all they had to do was log on to the Internet with products and innovations provided by the House of Apple.

Be Inclusive

Be inclusive. Cultivate a symbiotic and satisfying relationship between cult leaders and cult followers that offers mutual satisfaction, accomplishment, success, and enlightenment.

THE HOUSE OF THE DEAD

Since the birth of commercial rock and roll, profit was based on album sales. In the minds of most music executives, therefore, concert tours were really just advertisements designed to promote record sales. The concert experience wasn't really thought of as a product in and of itself. In fact, most bands lost money on their tours and went to this expense only because their contracts demanded it, and it was considered the only way to sell records and make money in the long term.

This went a long way toward shaping the rock concert experience and defining the way in which music and musicians interacted with their audiences. Every show in every city was always the same, constructed with brand consistency in mind and designed to please the most people in the least amount of time. The song sets were identical, always relying heavily on the band's familiar hits peppered with a couple of new tunes in order to acquaint the audience with the next top-ten hit so fans would immediately rush out and buy the new record. The songs themselves were performed in exactly the same way every time, and even the encores were planned.

Tickets were sold through third parties like Ticketron and Ticketmaster in order to accelerate sales, encourage ticket scarcity, and guarantee lines around the block at every local record store. It was an exclusive rather than an inclusive process. And because the albums were the commodity, not the performance experience, bootleg recording at concerts was strictly prohibited.

Further, because tours were largely a money-losing proposition, concerts were tightly budgeted and scheduled. Tours were strategically booked, heavily controlled, and shows never ran long because the band that was playing in Columbus tonight had to be in Chicago tomorrow. This put rock stars in a realm somewhere above and beyond the rest of us, off somewhere on a bus or in a helicopter or an airplane on their way to somewhere else. The interaction between rock stars and their fans was minimal, reserved only for the lucky and privileged few. This exclusivity and distance fed the myth of the rock star, which increased demand and, therefore, once again, sold more records.

The Dead turned this on its ear, and not only did they make their concerts, rather than their records, the product of scale, they also went about their ticketing completely differently from the rest of the industry. Because they had come up out of the mailing list– and newsletter-driven California counterculture of the 1960s and 1970s, they set up their own ticket agency early on and made their ticketing practices inclusive as opposed to exclusive. Their audience heard directly from the band about the next big happening, and loyal fans were rewarded with priority seating and sneak peeks at possible future set lists. Everyone was encouraged to attend, whether or not they had a ticket.

Dead concerts were not tightly scheduled, but emerged organically and spontaneously. Further, they were about more than music. They were about joining together with fans to support local causes, engage in positive social and political action, and change the world. And because it was the sharing of an experience in the moment rather than the recording that was the commodity, bootleggers or "tapers" were not only tolerated but encouraged. The Dead were betting that giving their music away would ultimately be more profitable than selling it. And they turned to be very right.

Today, nearly fifty years after that first happening at Ken Kesey's Acid Test party, the Dead remain one of the most successful rock bands of all time, and millions of Dead Heads around the world still faithfully follow the leader, even though many of them weren't even born when Jerry Garcia died.

Harness the Power of the Outliers
TAKING THE FRINGE MAINSTREAM

The counterculture in Steve Jobs's youth was made up largely of the misfits, the weirdos, the social outcasts and the disaffected youth, the geniuses and the lunatics, who existed on the fringe, outside the mainstream of culture. They eschewed, therefore, anything that smacked of the establishment, including big government and the giants of industry who sacrificed all creativity, individuality, artistry, and humanity in the name of profit and mass production.

Jobs saw the awesome commercial potential of the fringe cult's ideals, shared passion, and engagement to make changes in the world on a local level. He also realized, however, that the counterculture was never going to realize its vision of a simpler, more organic and artistic, DIY utopia until it could find a way to make its voice heard over the dominant din of mainstream culture.

Newsletters and free newspapers, hand circulated free verse, and spontaneous be-ins just weren't going to cut it, so long as the establishment controlled all of the means of mass communication and therefore held all the cards when it came to the power of information. And waiting for the mainstream infrastructure to crumble was just taking too long. Eventually, the counterculture got tired, got older, and ultimately moved to the suburbs and voted for Ronald Reagan.

Jobs wanted to make a machine that would give the power of information to the people. His vision was to give the small artisan, the tiny food collective, the free-verse poet, the computer hobbyists club, the one-man garage band, and the lone voice in a crowd the power to speak on the same scale as the giants of industry and the deafening mainstream messaging.

In creating Apple, and the cult of Apple, Jobs didn't just create a successful computer company; he gave the counterculture a way to change the world from the inside out. Now, all the counterculture had to do in order to be heard was to log on to the Internet with products and innovations provided by the House of Apple.

Be Dedicated to Making the World a Better Place
THE HOMEBREW COMPUTER CLUB

There was something else taking hold in the California counterculture in the 1970s, which was an organic outgrowth of the Summer of Love but looked very, very different. Alongside the hippies and the yippies, the transcendentalists, and the free verse poets, there was also something called the Homebrew Computer Club. The HBCC was a ragtag community of genius technohippies who, like the Dead Heads, wanted to hang out, have fun, and collectively change the world through their shared creativity.

Instead of free love, free food farms, psychedelics, and protesting in the streets, the nerds were trying to change the world from the inside out, with the help of a homemade circuit board and a whole bunch of crude switches and lights all hooked up to a makeshift keyboard and an old black-and-white TV. While everybody else was dancing topless in the streets and getting back to nature, the nerds were quietly attempting to co-create a technological revolution, by inventing the very first people's PC.

The Homebrew Computer Club met once a week in what they called the People's Computer Center, which meant one of two places: club founder Gordon French's garage in Menlo Park or the bar at the Oasis grill on El Camino Real. Despite the differences in their methodology, not to mention their fashion sense, the nerds of the Homebrew Computer Club were inspired by the same principles as most of California youth counterculture: fun, freedom, innovation, artistry, anarchy, and rock and roll as well as the passionate exchange of shared knowledge, cooperation, and creativity.

Like the Dead Heads, the Homebrewers communicated directly with each other through newsletters and came together spontaneously and religiously to share their hobby of hooking up stuff to see if it would work. It was a weekly love-in for geeks to share what they were most passionate about—the free and open exchange of information through technological innovation and engagement with other people who were just like them.

Everything was shared at the Homebrew. They shared their wisdom, their talent, their work, and most important, they shared a common vision of a future technonirvana, where everybody, regardless of their circumstances, would have unlimited access to the power of information. These were the very first seeds of what would ultimately become today's Silicon Valley. Yes, it's true. The very first Silicon Valley success story was written by a garage band of like-minded visionaries, who believed in fun over profit, community over competition, sharing over selling, and who created a cult based on the belief that it was their shared humanity that could and would save the world.

STATE-OF-THE-ART CULTS

Here are some other examples of successful sharing economy companies, who are using culting to build faithful followings for their brands.

Zappos

Zappos, the online shoe and apparel retailer—which incidentally also came out of the northern California youth counterculture—is dedicated to the cause of delivering happiness at any cost. Zappos, which began as a grassroots experiment based on a rave guest list, has amassed a devoted following of footwear fanatics since its founding in 1999, largely because they have made customer service their religion. The Zappos congregation are drawn to the brand's dedication to do anything and everything to make all their wishes come true and to deliver them happiness, which has resulted in a passionate brand following and fans who have an almost religious enthusiasm for the company.

The company has proclaimed ten commandments that have made them such a successful cult brand, which just sold to Amazon for $1.2 billion.

1. Deliver WOW through service.

2. Embrace and drive change.

3. Create fun and a little weirdness.

4. Be adventurous, creative, and open-minded.

5. Pursue growth and learning.

6. Build open and honest relationships with communication.

7. Build a positive team and family spirit.

8. Do more with less.

9. Be passionate and determined.

10. Be humble.

Red Bull

Red Bull is an extreme sport– and high energy–driven aspirational cult that creates experiences of mass scale based on the ability of the human spirit and the human body to triumph over obstacles and reach for the stars. Its latest campaign, which featured Felix Baumgartner skydiving from space, was a communal celebration of humanity's exploration of the final frontier. Red Bull is not selling an energy drink but a religion based on the amazing capabilities of the collective human imagination and energy. They are virtually "giving us wings."

Tough Mudder

Tough Mudder, the new fitness cult, transforms old-school obstacle courses into canvases of athletic prowess and personal expression where teams with colorful names like Daisy's Midnight Runners come together to test their mettle in athletic contests steeped in mud that recall the gladiator days of old.

Anonymous

Anonymous is a cult based on the religion of transparency, anonymity, and the right of the people to know the facts. Born out of the same impulses that prevailed at the Homebrew Computer Club, Anonymous bands hackers and activists together in collective social action, using the power of information and technology to expose injustice worldwide.

HOMEBREW YOUR OWN CULT REMINDERS

- Cult brands have to be created at a grassroots level and must be based on something that inspires passion and group participation.

- It's in our nature to want to identify and belong to a group of people who feel and think the same way we do. So there must be an entire culture and a community surrounding the brand based on the personality of the niche group that is sharing and co-creating it.

- Cults must have built-in opportunities for passionate engagement on a mass scale that will convert customers into evangelists who spread the gospel and recruit new followers.

- Cult brands should be irreplaceable in the lives of their followers. True customer loyalty is not only about getting a customer to consistently choose your brand over another; it's about getting that customer to always believe, come what may, and not even imagine life outside the cult.

- A cult brand has to be a little edgy, different, controversial, off center, and exist somewhat outside of the mainstream. Cults often choose microbrands that offer artisanal, organic, and handmade products and services that reflect a new ideology and way of being.

- Cult brands are not just about products and services. To many of their followers, they are a living, breathing surrogate family filled with like-minded individuals. They are a support group that just happens to sell products and services.

- There should be a symbiotic and satisfying relationship between cults and cult followers that offers mutual satisfaction, accomplishment, success, and enlightenment.

- Cults need to have a bold, innovative, charismatic, and committed leader who has sacrificed for the cause and has a vision for the future and the world that is in keeping with the ideologies and sensibilities of the congregation.

- Cults are inclusive and welcome everyone with a pure heart and a kindred spirit to come worship, participate, and co-create with the members.

- Cult brands promote personal freedom and draw power from their haters.

7.

Profit with Purpose

*We will dance when our laws command us to dance,
we will feast when our hearts desire to feast. Do we
ask the white man, "Do as the Indian does"? No,
we do not. Why, then, will you ask us, "Do as the
white man does"? It is a strict law that bids us to
dance. It is a strict law that bids us to distribute our
property among our friends and neighbors. It is a
good law. Let the white man observe his law; we shall
observe ours. And now, if you are come to forbid us
to dance, begone; if not, you will be welcome to us.*

—Chief O'waxalagalis of the Kwagu'ł
to anthropologist Franz Boas

In today's We-Commerce world, brands are under pressure to
learn how to profit in ways that provide for the collective good
as well as for their own bottom line. Increasingly, companies

are being asked by their target communities to offer value that extends beyond their product or service and to lead the way forward, toward a shared future abundance.

Studies show that consumers globally are making purchasing decisions based largely on what a company stands for and what a company does for the communities in which it operates. The actual goods and services that it produces are becoming less important as technology continues to level the playing field, democratizing creativity and making new Aha! moments and products a dime a dozen.

This truly is the age of brand republics who profit with purpose, and companies today must learn how to think, act, and plan the same way that towns, cities, and countries do, making decisions based on the common good, guided by their collective desire to provide a better quality of life for every citizen. In other words, ironically, the for-profit sector needs to start to think like the not-for-profit sector in order to profit long term. Businesses have to learn how to give back as part of their central business model, and this will have a revolutionizing effect on the culture and on the economy of the world going forward.

GIFT ECONOMIES

The notion of a culture and an economy centered on community benefit and sharing, as opposed to individual acquisition of wealth, is not new. In fact, gift economies have existed for thousands of years, and were the centerpiece of many of the most successful indigenous tribes of North America. There is perhaps no clearer illustration of a gift economy than the feast of the potlatch, which was the economic centerpiece of some Native American tribes. The practice persisted in secret long after it was outlawed by the U.S. and Canadian governments because without it, the intertribal culture and economy for those communities would have collapsed.

In potlatch economies and gift cultures, goods and services are given away rather than sold or traded. Power and success are measured by how much wealth you relinquish to others or even outright destroy, rather than how much you retain and protect. In this system, wealth is redistributed throughout the tribe through lavish ceremonial festivals of giving that were so powerful and counterintuitive to the Europeans that the federal government banned the potlatch festivals for almost a century. Nevertheless, the potlatches continued even through the Great Depression; those ceremonies, in fact, made it possible for the marginalized tribes to survive through difficult times in the same way they had for centuries—by sharing what they had with the rest of their community and with their neighbors.

Traditionally, only a chief could hold a potlatch. So giving away wealth was a luxury reserved exclusively for the elite. Potlatch feasts were held to mark and celebrate important events in the life of the chief. For the notables of a tribe, births, naming and coming of age ceremonies, weddings, and deaths all required a potlatch. Families would store up their wealth for years in order to be able to give away the most at these landmark moments because the relationships established through giving at the potlatch would determine the quality of their life with their tribe and neighboring chiefs from that day forward.

Potlatch feasts were extravagant events, packed full of food and music and grand ceremony, and they went on for days. Gifts given away at a potlatch included money, titles, blankets, copper, kettles, dishes, flour, and even furniture. Gifts were distributed according to rank, with the ranking guests getting the most gifts, which the chiefs would then redistribute among their own communities.

The potlatch was a seamless marriage of culture and commerce, with sharing and altruism as the cornerstone of social and commercial life. In addition, the potlatch brought about agreement, acceptance, and accord among tribal members, established trust in the observance of time-honored customs that guided social life, forged and renewed peaceful and mutually beneficial relationships between neighboring cultures, and obligated and intimidated enemies.

The potlatch made everything in the life of a tribe official: property boundaries, rights to natural resources, rights of inheritance, the addition of a new family member, or the loss of an old one. When change and disruption occurred in a gift tribe, the potlatch brought the tribal world together to eat, celebrate, accept the inevitable changes of life—good and bad—and give and receive the gifts that change brings.

THE PRINCIPLES OF POTLATCH FOR BRANDS

Companies today can learn a lot from the potlatch gift econ-omies, whose business model was uniquely designed to with-stand rapid change and disruption, and through a collective definition of wealth and success, endure as an integrated culture.

Like the chiefs who amassed wealth only to redistribute in order to increase their power, brands have to share the abundance; take some tips from Native Americans about how to put trust, sharing, and even a little ceremony at the center of their mission; and learn how to profit by providing for the wellbeing of their own and their surrounding com-munities.

Position Yourself to Accommodate $2-a-Day Economies

As the world's center of gravity continues to move from west to east, businesses will need to focus on what's being dubbed the *$2-a-day economies* if they expect to grow over the long term. The $2-a-day economies are those portions of the world that have risen above poverty (defined by areas in which citizens subsist on $1 a day or less) and, while still financially insecure, are growing into a new global middle class. It is in these emerging middle-class economies that the demand for goods and services will reside in the years to come.

So it's incumbent on brands to invest in the development

of these markets, so that they can achieve greater and greater power as consumers. Tomorrow's companies, in other words, will do well only if their customers do well. This means grassroots efforts that directly benefit communities in the short term, will benefit brands in the long term. Business development in today's $2-a-day economies is as much about infrastructure development, such as power and water, as it is about the delivery of products and services.

As a result, it is clear that today companies can no longer just check the box in the corporate social responsibility (CSR) realm through philanthropy or environmental responsibility. They must work to create what's being termed *shared value ecosystems* with the global business landscape at large.

Obey the Laws of the Triple Bottom Line

In the wake of these tectonic shifts in the topography of the market, a new principle of triple profitability or triple bottom line (3BL) is emerging. The triple bottom line, first fully explained by John Elkington in his 1997 book *Cannibals with Forks*, is a bottom line that measures both profits and the organization's impact on people and on the planet. The 3BL is a way of expressing a company's impact and sustainability on local and global scales.

The concept behind the triple bottom line is that companies are responsible to all their stakeholders, and stakeholders include everyone who is involved with the company, whether directly or indirectly, as well as the planet we're all living on.

This approach sees shareholders as part of the stakeholder group, but only one branch of it.

THE 3BL MODEL OF PROFITABILITY

In a 3BL business model, companies are required to deliver value in three distinct tiers:

- **Economic profitability:** Providing consistent positive earnings and long-term value to share-holders.

- **Social profitability:** The creation of purposeful contributions to society at large and the communities an organization serves through the power of its business.

- **Environmental profitability:** The proactive investment in technologies and other means that aim to serve, advance, and protect the natural world we live in.

THE 3BL IN ACTION: PEPSI REFRESH

Indra Nooyi, the CEO of PepsiCo, launched the ground-breaking Pepsi Refresh campaign in 2010, designed to put sustainable innovation and business development at the heart of Pepsi's culture. Using their marketing budget, rather than foundation dollars typically assigned to philanthropic efforts,

PepsiCo awarded $20 million in grants to individuals, businesses, and organizations who had an idea that would have a positive impact on their communities. Contestants were able to apply for a grant online, and the application process did not require any prior experience in grant writing, which made the process democratic and inclusive. Grants were given in the areas of health, arts and culture, food and shelter, the planet, neighborhoods, and education.

This campaign helped the company's mission to stretch way beyond making snacks and drinks to helping fuel global entrepreneurialism through the advancement of initiatives for everything from improved global health to clean water. Everything the company did from that point forward was designed to allow a burgeoning first-ever global middle class to consume goods and become participating citizens of the newly flattened world.

Pepsi Refresh demonstrates that tomorrow's success and growth depends on embedding the support and development of your brand communities right into your business model.

Place Benevolence at the Heart of Your Business

As per usual with revolutionary concepts, a decade ago the idea of business embracing a sharing economy and placing benevolence at the center of the strategies seemed out of the box and naive. A number of important trends, however, are beginning to support the need for organizations to become benevolent:

- Many organizations are critically dependent on hiring, motivating, and retaining good people in order to achieve success. In recent times, this notion has come to extend to the people they serve as well as the people that they employ.

- In many parts of the world, particularly in certain industries, good people are in short supply, as are critical resources. For companies to cultivate a workforce and a consumer base, they have to put resources into the development of these communities on a fundamentally human level.

- Different generations have different attitudes to work. While earlier generations may have tolerated impoverished conditions at work, people in the millennial generation are likely to be looking for more meaning. Unless they find this meaning, they'll move on.

- Consumers and potential recruits have many more choices than they had in the past and are more aware of the ethical and environmental stance of large companies. Many base their purchasing and career decisions on these considerations.

BUSINESS BENEVOLENCE IN ACTION: COKE (THRED)

In 2012, Coca-Cola Company announced the launch of (THRED), a free-to-play mobile game that is a joint project between Coca-Cola and (RED). (THRED) was developed to raise awareness and funds for the fight to end mother-to-child transmission of HIV by 2015. The collaboration between Coca-Cola and the (RED) project is a shining example of ethical consumerism in motion. A big brand, driven primarily by bottom line considerations, teams up with a brand guided by a primarily humanitarian mission, and both generate a profit and make the world a better place to live in. It's a win–win.

The (THRED) app helps raise money for the Global Fund to fight AIDS, Tuberculosis and Malaria—the world's leading financer of programs to fight these three diseases. Throughout the game, users have the opportunity to purchase power-ups and select items via in-app purchases. A percentage of the proceeds are donated to the Global Fund to invest in HIV/AIDS programs in Africa, including treatment for prevention of mother-to-child transmission of HIV.

(THRED) clearly demonstrates that big companies can be as agile as they want in the realm of producing lasting and meaningful change and benefit if they in fact choose to do so in ways that provide real value to a critical societal ailment, not just in ways that are convenient and aligned to the core business. By using their heft as an excuse to be hugely aspirational in their cause, curing AIDS globally, Coke took on a challenge as herculean as its brand and leveraged technology to set about making its dream a reality. (THRED) demonstrates that placing benevolence at the heart of your business model and addressing a vital societal need are critical for success in the global we-conomy.

Employ 3C Branding: Creativity, Collaboration, and Conscience

In the age of We-Commerce, capitalism is being pushed forward by another triumvirate: creativity, collaboration, and—the third C in the equation—conscience. In today's business climate, your success is not relevant or sustainable unless you are also giving back to the world in ways that are redemptive and restorative to all.

We have seen this sea change coming for years. First there was the Progressive Movement that began at the start of the twentieth century when companies aimed to leverage their resources to build better communities and help people access the resources needed to live better lives. Leading companies of the day like Johnson & Johnson and Avon even built these doctrines into their charters, and Henry Ford followed with the Model T. The car was not just disruptive for the business doctrines it helped create but for the accessibility it offered by producing a car for $300 as opposed to $3,000. This is the $2-a-day economy model's most notable ancestor.

Decades later this movement played out with the dawn of all things green in the early 2000s, when CSR was the catchall buzzword. Go green! Reduce your carbon foot-print! Make sustainability not a thing to do, but a part of your business strategy! Everything imaginable was done to show that a company was environmentally responsible.

Unfortunately, at the time, many other acts of irrespon-sibility were going on across corporate America that led to a whole new form of natural disaster. As a result of the 2008 financial collapse, corporate social responsibility has been reimagined to align with the new creatively collaborative economic landscape. Being responsible as a corporation now extends way beyond maintaining a mindful environ-mental footprint and toward an all-encompassing fusion of profit with purpose that has come to envelop the global business landscape. If a company is to truly succeed and lead for the long-term, the value that it creates for society must have many branches and be designed to both serve *and* protect.

CHIPOTLE: *FARMED AND DANGEROUS*

Chipotle Mexican Grill is notorious for shunning advertising agencies. In the words of co-CEO Steve Ells, "To be able to build a brand, you need to be yourself." Recognizing the dif-ficulty of working with an external agency, Chipotle has embraced an unconventional approach and built a devoted audience through savvy promotions and award-winning viral YouTube sensations. Most notably, Ellis had the world's favorite Mexican fast-casual joint create a television show.

It's called *Farmed and Dangerous*, and the four-episode miniseries debuted on Hulu on February 17, 2014.

Farmed and Dangerous takes a satirical look at the controversy and extreme measures that are often associated with industrial-produced foods and vegetables in the era of "monster fruit." By creating this series, Chipotle addressed a heavy issue head-on, while also demonstrating their deep legacy commitment to using farm-to-table, high-end sustainable ingredients in all that they do. They also helped pioneer the movement of brands from producers of goods and services to purveyors of real and meaningful content and experiences that not only engage but also entertain. Chipotle demonstrated the need for winning brands to create experiences that serve to delight and connect with consumers in ways that transcend transactional experiences. With the studio approach to programming that addresses a meaningful issue facing consumers and the world at large, Chipotle shows both its commitment to being among the world's top fast casual dining restaurants as well as a leading global corporate citizen.

WHOLE FOODS

Whole Foods' mission as outlined by its visionary CEO John Mackey is not to sell more food or merely reimagine the grocery store experience. Whole Foods has set out to change the way the world eats, with the goal of eliminating killers like cancer and heart disease that are so influenced by the Western diet.

And, true to form, their mission begins at home, trying to bring healthy lifestyles to their own employees, who have become brand ambassadors through experience with the company's mission. Whole Foods pays for four hundred employees a year to attend a weeklong retreat intended to improve their health. The company also gives employees financial incentives to score well on biometric assessments of their health. It recently opened its first medical and wellness clinic, where employees can receive primary medical care at no cost, along with health coaching. In the stores themselves, Whole Foods recently instituted a rating system to identify the healthiest foods for customers.

Mackey is a pioneer in reimagining the role that companies and their chief executives ought to play in the lives of their communities that extends far beyond the bottom line. In fact, he not only has turned his company into the modern example of corporate innovation and goodness but also is sharing his vision with others through his Conscious Capitalism conference.

More than 180 chief executives attend the Conscious Capitalism CEO Summit each year since its inception. Speakers at the most recent event included the chief executives of companies like Hyatt Hotels, Home Depot, and Panera Bread. Organizers expect well over 200 attendees for the next summit.

Whole Foods teaches us that today brands and entrepreneurs can become republics that are engines of profitability for shareholders and for the communities they serve.

They can also become agents for spreading the positive ideals that help people globally to rally around a mission to make the world a better place.

THE TRIPLE A STANDARD FOR TOMORROW'S LEADING BRAND REPUBLICS

Alignment: Align your business with your core values as well as the values of your consumers, your community, and the planet. As the age of We-Commerce unfolds, leading brands will have increased responsibility not only for the shareholders and employees they retain but for the world we all live in.

Authenticity: Attach yourself to issues and causes that are authentic to your business and your region. Through collaboration with competitors and complementary business partners, find ways to drive toward positive triple bottom line results in ways that benefit the collective we and yield profit with clear purpose. As purchasing decisions today are being based on what a company stands for, it becomes critical for leading organizations to move beyond talking the talk and really walk the walk.

Action: Whether you're starting up a business designed to benefit the collective we from inception or are carving out a long-term 3BL strategy for a legacy brand, it's action that will speak far louder than words. This phenomenon is not regional but global and will only continue to rise in significance. Smart brands will understand the weight of this new paradigm and act accordingly, and they will create the necessary scale required for putting their money where their mouths are on a globalized basis.

PROFIT WITH PURPOSE REMINDERS

- Be the change you are looking for in the world.

- Content and context are king.

- Place benevolence at the heart of your brand.

- Develop and support your brand communities.

- Do what you can to foster a growing global middle class.

- Put dollars into infrastructure to make the lives of your constituents better.

- Do what is right, not just what is convenient for your brand.

8.

Bespoke Is the New Beautiful

be spoke
bə'spōk/ adjective
Definition: custom or made to order

It's hard to imagine considering the soggy and ubiquitous sugar roll that it ultimately became, but in its heyday the Danish was the pastry of presidents, handmade by four-star chefs, all trained at the prestigious Danish Culinary Studio on Fifth Avenue in New York.

There is some controversy over who can actually claim the invention of the Danish, probably because it became a global success story and everybody wants a little bit of credit for such a delicious development in Western history. Regardless of its true origins, however, the Danish became the height of elegance when it made its way to America by way of a chef named Lauritz Klitteng, who baked the pastry for Woodrow Wilson's wedding in 1915. As a result, the Danish became an overnight American success story and the de rigueur pastry at society brunches coast to coast.

The Lincoln Continental was also the height of American luxury in its day, reserved for the rich, the powerful, and the famous. Originally designed as a one off as Edsel Ford's personal vehicle, Lincolns were small batch, handmade, designed by renowned artists, and so innovative and luxurious that they even outpaced the Rolls Royce in prestige and price. The first commercial Lincoln Continental, produced in 1938, is still considered one of the most beautiful cars in the world. The next generation Lincoln Continental Mark II, first produced in 1955, had the highest quality control ever seen in the automobile industry. Despite the high price, Ford actually lost money on every vehicle sold, because the fine production and hand fabrication were so costly. This did not seem to matter to Ford, who had seemingly produced an automotive masterpiece simply to prove that they could and to show the world how magnificent and luxurious an American-made car could be. The experiment was an epic global success. The Continental Mark II was sold for just two model years, with about three thousand total units built. Because they were in such short supply, there was a velvet rope system for buyers.

Sadly, like so many other handcrafted iconic objects of

historic significance and unrivaled quality, the Lincoln and the Danish became so popular and commoditized that they became ubiquitous, mundane, and ordinary. All the bespoke artistry, passion, and élan were gone. The Lincoln ultimately became the Ford Taurus before disappearing entirely. And the Danish went from a meticulously handcrafted pastry to a soggy, sugar-saturated bun in a bag.

As goes the Lincoln and the Danish, so goes the world. But now, I'm happy to report, in the dawning era of small and bespoke as the new beautiful, the Danish and the Lincoln are returning to the luxury of their past, revisiting their handmade artisanal roots but with a modern twist. Local bakeries, food trucks, and Michelin-rated chefs alike are once again embracing the artistry of the Danish, using techniques from multicultural flavor fusion to molecular gastronomy, and the Lincoln is returning to its origin, calling on well-known artists and craftspeople to create a new generation of best-in-class luxury car that invokes its respected heritage.

The resurgence of interest in the bespoke brilliance of the Danish and the Lincoln illustrates that in today's we-conomy a hyperspecific focus on craftsmanship and precision and doing one thing better than anybody else in the world is a great recipe for success.

RULES FOR BRANDS WHEN SMALL
IS THE NEW BIG
Don't Become Too Big to Succeed

Following the 2008 financial meltdown when the adage "Too big to fail" was more overused than the word *selfie*, a sea change began to take shape: the idea of bigger no longer meant better. In the wake of the collapse of Lehman and the other enormous financial institutions driving Wall Street, the idea of staying small has come into vogue. Today, it's important for companies to focus on bespoke goods and services and staying small in order to win trust and consumer loyalty.

The banking industry was perhaps the first to realize the need for smaller and sleeker entities that could be more easily regulated and held accountable. A huge shift in consumer attitudes toward smaller and more regional banks took hold with new leaders such as Umpqua and Banco Popular rising to fame. Investment banks even jumped on the bandwagon with a slew of top bankers leaving the hallowed halls of financial giants like Goldman and Bank of America to start their own banking boutiques. These boutiques were designed to leverage personal reputation and industry expertise in order to create a new kind of deal market and new relationships with their customers based on collaboration and transparency. In fact in 2010, most major deals were done by investment boutiques, leaving the big boys eating their dust, scrambling to find a way to live another day.

Develop Couture Communications

In a sea of giant communication conglomerates like Inter-Public Group Media Brands (IPG) and WPP with ships so enormous it was impossible to shift their direction quickly, an opportunity arose for the arrival of some smaller competitors who could offer both the agility required in a 24/7 news cycle and a niche focus, not a one-size-fits-all model. Smaller firms like Crispin Porter + Bogusky (CPB) and Weiden+Kennedy began to flood the market with revolutionary campaigns (outlined in the following sections) that reinvented advertising as an enhancement to, rather than an interruption of, life's programming. Boutique firms like those mentioned took center stage, forcing industry titans like McCann, Grey, and Saatchi to regroup and closely examine the dramatically altered playing field in order to figure out how to regain relevance.

From cars to cuisine, gaming to glasses, the Small Is the New Big mandate ushered in the era of bespoke production and procurement that has given way to the age of collaborative commerce we are living in today.

BOUTIQUE BLOCKBUSTERS

CPB—Baby Carrots: CPB transformed a vegetable into an orange snack food that rivaled the standing orange champions Doritos and Cheetos, turning the baby carrot industry into a sector worth literally billions. A group of farmers got together to launch a $25 million ad campaign aimed at making packaged baby carrots cool. The idea was that kids may eat more of them if they can think of carrots as a kind of junk food. Basically a campaign was concocted to redefine healthy, as opposed to merely sell vegetables.

Carrots were featured in extreme stunts and placed into vending machines among other innovative techniques designed to put baby carrots at the epicenter of cool food culture.

The result? Five years of continued industry growth, with carrots often viewed as the new chips and getting dunked into everything from hummus to habanero salsa.

Weiden+Kennedy—Smell Like a Man: Weiden+Kennedy's Old Spice campaign Smell Like a Man took a brand that was associated with fathers and grandfathers and made it into a must-have toiletry for young men, winning an Emmy for Outstanding Commercial in 2010 in the process. Being a seventy-three-year-old brand, Old Spice had long been marked as a product your grandfather would use. Attempting to change this, Procter & Gamble hired Wieden+Kennedy and together they came up with a campaign that would not only change the Old Spice brand but invent the new era of viral marketing. The campaign was revolutionary because although it aired during the Super Bowl, it was like a cat with nine lives, being applauded, parodied, laughed at, and engaged with across the social media landscape for not just months but years. The Old Spice campaign not only changed the face of advertising but popularized the idea of brands telling continuing stories, moving from mere purveyors of product to purveyors of truly engaging and immersive content. The ads were a harbinger of the arrival of brands as the studios of tomorrow.

The original ad launched in 2010 and five years later the kooky and funny tales of men and their fragrance live on. Their latest nature-themed take on humorous advertisement aired to critical acclaim and undoubtedly yet another new generation of devout Old Spice loyalists was born.

The Warby Wow Factor: Warby Parker is a small eye-wear company started by four young college friends and dedicated to addressing the needs of the one billion people worldwide who don't have access to eyeglasses. Warby has quickly become an iconic brand as a result of its mission to offer high-quality and stylish eyewear, in engaging environments, at affordable prices. In addition, Warby is committed to maintaining a net zero carbon footprint and providing eye care and glasses to the developing world. Warby is now commanding a big market share of their industry, at the expense of larger, more expensive and established brands, and was recently valued at $500 million.

Pages from Billee's Playbook

In 1994, I became the U.S. press secretary for the government of the Philippines at a small PR firm in New York City called the Icon Group. In that capacity, my job was to show-case the democracy that President Fidel V. Ramos and his cabinet were bringing to the country and all of the terrific investment opportunities for U.S. businesses that came along with it. At the time, the focus was on an English-speaking workforce and low-cost labor because the Southeast Asian region was viewed by most as the third world. While regions like Indonesia and Singapore were slowly on the rise, most countries in Southeast Asia were known for their civil unrest, martial law, and incidents of canings for the slightest infractions, like chewing gum. While my work to showcase the Philippines and its new menu of attractions was covered by the top tier business press globally, the region was many years away from being viewed as an epicenter of innovation.

Fifteen years later when I landed in Singapore to handle on-the-ground executive and brand communications for Honeywell Aerospace at the newly acclaimed Singapore air show, I was floored at how much things had changed. What I found now was one of the most advanced airports and business infrastructures in the world. It was at this time that I recognized that the dialogue on what frontier economies could bring to the game would soon extend beyond costs and communication to industry and development.

As a result of this dynamic shift, I began to implement a hyperlocalized, bespoke approach to corporate narrative communications designed to foster meaningful dialogues, told through a local lens with a human emphasis on culture.

BESPOKE IS THE NEW BEAUTIFUL

At the airshow, we showcased Honeywell as a leading provider of cutting edge cockpit technologies but also introduced their corporate leadership—local people who intimately understood the power of the region as an incubator for true innovation.

We told this story to global business press through one uniform narrative with a singular voice, and then worked with local offices to customize the message to speak specifically to the targeted regions, in their own language and vernacular. The result was a powerful and compelling communications campaign that positioned Honeywell as the leading light helping to produce the world's best aviation technologies and doing so in a way that fosters growth in the frontier economies that will forever change the face of global commerce.

Today, in a global we-conomy, it is more important than ever to engage new and emerging markets with effective bespoke, artisanal communications techniques, such as these pivotal considerations:

1. Impactful storytelling coming from a central narrative, yet customized by region.

2. The need to add a level of humanity to all storytelling in ways that transform communications from statements of facts to meaningful dialogues.

3. The rising opportunity of artful storytelling and business artistry to conquer new frontiers, while also nurturing their development.

Go from DIY to DIT (Do It Together)

In today's collaborative business landscape, the DIY and makers movement has expanded beyond the thrill of doing something yourself to encompass the jubilant experience of doing things together.

DIT defines a collective action that benefits a community, as opposed to a single person. By moving from DIY to DIT, we can encourage more people to act in a more inclusive community-centric fashion. This does not stem from technology; it grows out of the power of creating a movement powered by like-minded individuals around a common goal or theme.

DIT DALLAS

Dallas experienced a major downturn in the arts in the first decade of the century due to the global economic recession. Just as in many other major urban areas, art was the first thing to go because of economic constraints. Dallas decided to pull together and do something about it and founded the Socialized Contemporary Artists Bureau (S.C.A.B.). Artists from all over Dallas, and from all over the country once the word got out, began to work together along with art lovers in the community to build a new and vibrant visual arts community in Dallas. What resulted looked very different from a gallery space, because the installations and the settings for those installations were being created by the artists themselves.

Pop-up and temporary spaces dominated the landscape, and art shows were going up in all kinds of unorthodox spaces like warehouses and loading docks. This energy became infectious. What started as a couple dozen emerging artists with no place to show their art has led to a statewide, and sometimes even national, conversation about whether Dallas can be a world-class arts city.

Other examples of DIT can be found everywhere across the nation, as the central idea is based largely on the American ideals of freedom and charting your own destiny together, as a community. DIT embraces a creative and self-organizing entrepreneurial spirit by creating diverse, resilient, and thriving community ecosystems.

The DIT revolution is at the heart of the new age of We-Commerce, bringing people of diverse cultures and areas of focus together to create something together that is greater than anything that could be created in isolation. As business leaders today, we must all be aware of the importance of building effective teams, whose sum productivity will be greater than that of their individual parts.

BESPOKE IS THE NEW
BEAUTIFUL REMINDERS

- Customize and hyperlocalize communications in emerging markets.

- Create unique retail experiences that incorporate the neighborhood or the region.

- Stay small but include all.

- Bigger is better is dead. Sleekness and the agility of the small rules the marketplace today.

- Do it together for the many, not alone for the few.

- Bring the spirit of art and handmade craftsmanship into your business, no matter how big your brand.

9.

Stay Small but Reach All

Staying small is not just about the scale of your business; it's about the size of your products, the environments within which you produce and distribute your products, and the settings within which they are purchased or consumed. In an era of digital overload, where attention spans are constantly being competed for, a sense of chaos and unrest often ensues. Items and services that can be easily engaged with, attached to, or immersed in by appealing to consumers on as individual a level as possible are the path forward for brand communications.

As a result, executives inside big companies as well as lone entrepreneurs in start-ups are all chasing the same goal: pairing the agile innovation and bespoke goods and services of the small brands with the expansive and cohesive reach of the big companies. In other words, they want to have their cake and eat it too. It's the best of both worlds.

So how have small brands, started by a handful of individuals on a shoestring budget, managed to succeed so quickly, rivaling the reach and profits of their big brand competitors? And how have well-known corporations of significant size managed to foster sleek "intrapreneurial" groups inside their large organizational structures?

STRATEGIES FOR MAINTAINING SCALE WHILE REALIZING GROWTH
Remember That Even Big Companies Can Be Small

Many of us tend to assume that big companies are anti-entrepreneurial dinosaurs that resist change, but history teaches us otherwise. Corporations have been running entrepreneurship-type programs for many years with much success.

The most notable is the esteemed Lockheed Martin Skunk Works—a small group of employees working on revolutionary products, such as famous aircraft designs including the U-2 and the SR-71 Blackbird. Even today, some companies still refer to innovative test projects as "Skunk Works projects."

Large companies are starting new entrepreneurship initiatives because they need fuel for innovation, desire top talent, and need to sustain a competitive advantage. Smart companies are catering to inventive employees, allowing workers to pitch ideas, and even funding the viable ones. They are holding entrepreneurship contests, investing in start-ups and bringing on entrepreneurs-in-residence because they realize that all companies have to think like small businesses in order to survive, no matter how big or well established they are.

Nurture Intrapreneurship

In the past, we've heard of intrapreneurs in the context of all-star engineers working within major corporations, who would come up with original ideas and create new products. These days, companies have embraced intrapreneurship as a core business competency and put a culture and systems in place to encourage start-up style within even very large and established corporate brands.

Google is a great supporter of this trend. Its Intrapreneurship Program has launched initiatives designed specifically to encourage ingenuity and creative thinking. Google's Innovation Time Off encourages its employees to spend 20 percent of their work time on projects that interest them and which they think will benefit Google and their customers.

If you work at Google, you are working in a big company that is instilling a start-up culture. This is part of the reason they receive thousands of résumés each day. Intrapreneurship programs are promising because they cater to employees who are entrepreneurial in spirit but lack the resources to go out on their own. Both the employee and the company can benefit from the partnership.

INTRAPRENEURIAL ALL-STARS

Here are two outstanding examples of intrapreneurship at work within both companies.

Shutterstock

Every year, Shutterstock hosts an annual twenty-four-hour hack-a-thon for their employees. These challenges are designed to allow team members to pursue any ideas they have that would make the company better, encouraging their talent to collaborate, create, and innovate together on behalf of the brand. Shutterstock used this type of initiative to create several critical platform enhancements. Most notable is Oculus—a data analysis tool that came out of the 2012 hack-a-thon and is now used at Shutterstock every day.

3M

The 3M Company, often called the godfather of intrapreneurship, essentially invented the model with the completely accidental advent of the Post-It. Spencer Silver, a scientist at 3M, was attempting to create an extremely strong adhesive to use in aerospace technology. Instead, he accidentally created a light adhesive that stuck to surfaces well but didn't leave a nasty residue. After many years of persistence and spreading the word about his discovery it finally clicked with another 3M scientist, Art Fry. He and Silver began to develop a product together. Post-It notes were born, and if you are one of the vast majority of desk workers you're probably looking at a pad of them right now. The 3M story shows that sometimes intrapreneurship happens by chance, so it pays build a culture that encourages it.

Encourage Artistry in Residence

In 2013, Billy Joel became the first artist in residence at Madison Square Garden. This pairing infused a new artistic and creative energy into two brands that are . . . mature, to say the least. The end result? Sixteen and counting sold out back-to-back shows for Joel at the Garden, over a period spanning two years.

Today, leading companies have embraced the idea of artists- and entrepreneurs-in-residence to create their own brand of bespoke business artistry and innovation. These programs help companies big and small keep their eye on the most critical aspect of the small business ethos: the notion that art should always be married with commerce to drive, with laser precision, toward the ideas, creations, and technologies that make us better but not necessarily more immediately profitable.

Google is a prime example of a behemoth that has

leveraged the idea of in-house specialization to stay ahead of the curve and to advise them on start-ups. Stacy Brown-Philpot has been one of the most notable entrepreneurs-in-residence at Google Ventures. While Stacy never started her own business, she has led operations for more than forty different products, including Google Search, Chrome, and Google+.

Facebook also has an active and ongoing residence program. It's among the most innovative corporate programs of its kind. Now in its second year, the program has made artists a regular fixture around the Facebook campus. Facebook's longer term vision is to demonstrate that a workplace filled with art and with access to artists can actually benefit a company in tangible ways, particularly with respect to how much employees value working there and how productive they are. It's not that the art fades into the background, but rather it becomes the gathering place for new thought and creativity throughout the company. Artistry is the new company watercooler.

Artist-in-residence programs clearly demonstrate the new relationship between art and commerce in today's we-conomy. And as these programs illustrate, everyone benefits from this new mash-up. Corporate employees and brands have found a way to suffuse their culture, products, and services with art and creativity, and artists have found a new generation of patrons to bolster their expressive efforts.

Crowdsource Innovation

The rapid exchange of data necessary to stay competitive today demands that brands have access to multiple, fluid sources of information. Crowdsourcing uses the input of the public or brand community to resolve strategic problems or complete tasks that normally would have been addressed internally. Widely dispersed contributors acquired through an open call for participation are asked to offer opinions on how to accomplish a specific objective. Open innovation for new products or improvement to existing products is also generally encouraged.

Crowdsourcing participants can come from anywhere and everywhere, giving companies a wide and comprehensive view of the response to their initiatives. Today's mobile functionality has made the dialogue between a brand and its constituency truly global in scope and gives even small brands a reach and scale that would only have been dreamed about in the past.

KINGS OF CROWD SOURCING
Anheuser-Busch: Black Crown

The world's leading brewer has applied crowdsourcing to enormous advantage. While Budweiser is easily America's best-selling king of beers, AB sought customer input to develop a brand more attuned to craft-beer tastes than their mainstream labels. The development of Black Crown, a golden amber lager, combined a competition between company brew masters with consumer suggestions and tastings to develop a crowd-pleasing alternative brew. This project had more than twenty-five thousand consumer collaborators.

In Brazil, where AB markets the leading brand, Skol, it has opened Poptent, a crowdsourced video-production company specializing in TV commercials that utilizes a social network of thirty-five thousand videographers from 120 nations. AB's site offers potential collaborators a range of opportunities with the firm.

Nokia: IdeasProject

Like most crowdsourcing ventures, Nokia's IdeasProject defines itself as a global community devoted to open innovation. The IdeasProject focuses on consumer-derived collaboration across 210 nations to improve the viability of Nokia products in all markets.

The IdeasProject is valuable because it draws on the consumer experiences of participants to generate new ideas about the kind of products they seek from Nokia. Crowdsourcing collaborators are enabled and empowered, becoming their own agents of product design. Nokia shares revenues generated from crowdsourced ideas with IdeasProject participants. This idea of paying consumers for their ideas, including them not only creatively but financially in a brand's success and effectively making the world part of the company on some level, really shows us how ubiquitous and powerful the notion of sharing has become in the we-conomy.

Infodio

Infodio is a Cairo-based crowdsourced educational platform where anyone can record and listen to audio "cards" or sound bites that contain information. Think of Infodio as the intersection between Wikipedia and SoundCloud. Its vision is to create a platform where the world's knowledge is recorded in audio format, in different languages and available to everyone for free.

Infodio chose audio over video because audio makes it easier for people to create cards, as they don't need a camera, only a microphone. Also, audio uses much less bandwidth, which in turn allows the cards to be available to people with slow Internet connections.

Small Is the New Beautiful

The small is beautiful movement has been building steam for nearly half a century. When Schumacher first made the statement it resonated with a ding. When Seth Godin wrote about the topic in 2005, the ding became a growing siren. Today, nearly a decade later, the notion has become a clarion call to action.

Thinking small applies to scope, niche, and focus. The goal is to do just one thing and do that one thing better than anyone else. Jay Moskowitz's Peerless Wind Systems is a great example of this. Peerless is an artistic, highly energy-efficient vertical-axis wind turbine that has been created for use in urban environments, island nations, and emerging countries, where more than one billion people have little or no electricity. The patent-pending electric generator is a beautifully designed helix shape and can produce energy at very low wind speeds. Its special turbine drives the generator to deliver more energy than others of similar size. These turbines are the white Apple earbuds of energy: they have taken something functional and utilitarian and made it beautiful, beneficial to society, and unique.

STAY SMALL BUT EMBRACE ALL REMINDERS

- Nurture intrepreneurship and encourage innovation in your company whether you are small or large.

- Commission an artist-in-residence to introduce artistry and creativity into your corporate culture.

- Create do it together (DIT) projects that bring your employees and your consumers together in participatory acts of expression and social good.

- Make the world your idea bank by crowdsourcing new developments and asking your brand community to tell you what they think and want.

10.

Pop-Up-Alooza!

Through the pop-up shop, big business has harnessed the powerful culture and energy of small start-ups, and small start-ups have found new avenues to approach broader consumer markets. Pop-up shops are micro-stores that bring people together for limited periods of time to experience and engage with each other and with the brand's retail environment.

The pop-up shop is an increasingly popular model that allows new businesses to test their products with minimal infrastructure costs—because the shops are set up in existing spaces—while also gleaning invaluable consumer insights that can be critical in getting a product or other offering to reach its full potential. The principles behind this business practice align well with the age of collaborative consumption, where much of successful commerce and innovation stems from experiences that unite people around shared passions.

POP-UP ECONOMICS

Opening a storefront is not easy. Finding and funding the perfect space, building out the interior, and getting the right services to launch are formidable tasks. On top of that, most people can't afford to pay for a long-term lease, particularly small-business owners. So it makes financial sense to share the costs of space with other vendors who can benefit from pop-up environments. And it makes strong business sense, as this type of environment places brands directly at the intersection of the two most powerful vectors of economy: culture and commerce.

A common mistake, however, is considering these new economic vessels as canvases for young businesses or brick-and-mortar entities alone. E-commerce has grown up, and several brands that have built a following online are acting in reverse and migrating to the real world. Showrooms and pop-up shops are sprouting up in trendy neighborhoods, bringing along opportunities for online retailers to not only sell goods but also share their brand stories.

The first Amazon pop-up shop, which operated in New York during the 2014 holiday season, is a fantastic example of this. Amazon, arguably the top retail company in the world, acknowledged the power of a physical presence. That allowed them to close one potential chink in their armor by using reverse show rooming, where customers browse products on Amazon but then buy them at a live retail outlet.

Legacy brands are leveraging pop-up shops to refresh

the dialogue with old and new consumers alike. These alternative outlets allow them to engage their consumers in innovative ways that lead to deeper relationships built around emotional connections whose impact goes beyond just selling someone a product to satisfy a material need.

Pop-ups are also extraordinarily powerful due to the synergy that can result from having many complementary businesses located closely together in one space. For instance, a pop-up space might be filled by small businesses each made up of one or two owners selling wares like artisan jewelry, candles, or clothing, all of which appeal to a similar market and thus benefit by being sold in proximity to one another. Business owners can identify new product ideas and collaboration opportunities by working in a community instead of in isolation. These interactions can strengthen local economies and begin to create the new local ecosystems of innovation that will help drive the era of collaborative consumption. And, as our ever-more-connected world continues to evolve, pop-ups are helping to fuel new types of commerce globally as well.

Pop-Up Power Players
ADIDAS: STAN YOURSELF POP-UP

Pop-ups can be used in meaningful ways to introduce brands back into culture and reestablish connections with legacy consumers, while creating fresh dialogues with new markets. Pop-ups are authentic ways of engaging consumers in meaningful experiences that lead to long-term brand advocacy and participation.

Adidas has recently experienced a massive brand renaissance worldwide, and one of the tools they used to help them recapture their A-list status was the pop-up. Through the use of this new economic construct, the brand has slowly but surely regained a cultural position since the 1980s, when the acronym of their name was used as cool kid code for "All Day I Dream About Sex."

Designed to celebrate the launch of the company's Stan Smith collection (named for the pro tennis player), the London pop-up store included an interactive floor, a digital Stan Yourself station, and a 3D printing post. The Stan Yourself station allowed for customers to put their own faces on shoes, while the 3D printing post let them make custom lace locks.

The London shop was open for only three days in January 2014 but yielded acclaimed results and visibly reinvigorated interest in the brand worldwide.

HUBLOT: BIG BANG POP-UP

Pop-ups can be used on a global scale in targeted hyperlocal ways to connect with the middle class and elite consumers in frontier markets, eventually causing interest to trickle up to traditional markets.

Luxury watch designer Hublot located a pop-up in Singapore's Paragon Shopping Mall and featured over $20 million worth of merchandise. The store was created in collaboration with Singaporean designer Chris Lee. Titled Big Bang, the two-story installation featured black gems cascading from the ceiling. The much discussed retail space was open for only two weeks in 2012, yet garnered worldwide attention and introduced the brand as the luxury watch of the new global elite.

PORTUGAL: WARHOL POP-UP

Pop-ups can be used to create experiences that benefit brands by fostering meaningful interactions with their consumers, as well as to provide artistic value to the communities where they reside. Pop-ups can also serve as educational vehicles that help consumers understand the seismic shifts in culture and commerce taking place around the world.

The Lisbon-based company LIKEarchitects wanted to avoid the conventional white-walled museum space to showcase Andy Warhol's art and instead opted for an unusual design: the Warhol pop-up. The Warhol pop-up consisted of four rooms constructed out of a maze of fifteen hundred metal paint cans. It was located in the Colombo Shopping Mall's atrium from April to July 2013, and consisted of eight layers, the bottom three of which were filled with sand to keep the structure stable. The temporary retail space proved to be a hit—it attracted more than a hundred thousand visitors and lots of buzz in its short lifespan, a notable achievement and a signal of the global resurgence of Warhol's popularity.

WARBY PARKER: CLASS TRIP

Beyond creating beautiful showrooms, the Warby Parker Class Trip that launched in the summer of 2013 has been a benchmark in click-to-brick campaigns that is the envy of retail marketers everywhere. True to the Warby Parker brand, which places fashionable, reasonably priced eyewear in engaging retail settings, they retrofitted an old school bus and set out on a tour across America to share Warby Parker with everyone they could. They also used the Class Trip as an opportunity to shine a spotlight on their trendsetting customers via a dedicated website.

What's important to glean from Warby Parker's pop-up shop tour is that documenting every aspect of their campaign provided digital collateral to help fuel future projects. This is the founding principle of the BRANDthropologie Media (my company) production studio, Mojo Risin' Productions. The studio was created to curate brand life events in ways that transform singular occurrences into engaging and ultimately monetizable programming.

EBAY: KATE SPADE POP-UP

It's not every day that you see an eBay store anywhere but on eBay. So people were surprised to see their favorite eBay storefront, Kate Spade, transformed into a physical pop-up shop like no other. The window included a huge touch screen that stood ready to take your order and deliver your goods in less than an hour.

All of the marketing information gleaned from the pop-up was used to create a more customer-centric Kate Spade—one that knows what its consumers want, how they want it, when they want it, and how best to provide it to them. The companies also used the pop-up in a new way that showcased their business model for the entire sector and was dubbed the "retail store of the future." As eBay executive Healey Cypher stated, "We know how many people are walking by, and of those people who turn up square and look at the glass, that's a CPM (cost per thousand of impressions). That's an impression. Then if they touch it it's a CPC (cost per click). But then also the time that it takes to do these things, what happens between them, catalysts that get them to engage. If they buy it and schedule for delivery . . . When in the history of retail has a retailer ever had info about what's happening outside their walls, before transaction?"

FESTIVALMANIA

Festivals are a new form of pop-up culture that offers enormous opportunities for brands to reach their markets in engaging ways through an experience economy that stresses living in the moment over ownership and combines a collective physical experience with digital engagement.

Here is a roundup of festivals that your brand can engage with to meet the DIT movement head-on and start a whole new kind of conversation with carefully targeted new constituencies.

American Music Festival Hot List

The following is a list of the hottest music festivals in the country and the key lessons we can all take away from each.

SASQUATCH! MUSIC FESTIVAL

A groundbreaking festival aimed at creating a lasting experience as opposed to a mere event, Sasquatch! makes use of not just one but *two* holiday weekends. Split between Memorial Day and Fourth of July weekends, Sasquatch! presented two completely different lineups in 2014. The festival sold out in a mere ninety minutes last year and attracted acts as cool as OutKast, Violent Femmes, and De La Soul.

Sasquatch! teaches us that festivals can be used to reimagine cultural experiences that need rejuvenation. What person is not sick of parades on Memorial Day and fireworks on the Fourth of July? What Sasquatch! shows us is that brands can use festivals and other collaborative experiences to breathe new life into traditions and milestones that cry out for reinvention.

ELECTRIC DAISY CARNIVAL

The reenvisioned rave known as Electric Daisy Carnival is one of the few music festivals to take place on both coasts. The New York City event is a two-day warm-up for the bigger attraction, which is the insane party in Las Vegas. There is no electronic dance music festival that's more widely anticipated. And Electric Daisy does it right, having acts perform between sunset and sunrise as opposed to during the day.

Electric Daisy takes the glorious collaborative experiences of the past (disco and raves) and reimagines those longed-for and much missed cultural phenomena as sexy, modern celebrations. Electric Daisy shows brands the power of collective events, their multiregional appeal, and how effective it can be to blend the best of the old with the best of the new to drive true engagement and immersion.

BONNAROO

None of the other American festivals are as hardcore as Bonnaroo. It's one of the greatest festival camping experiences in the world and Bonnaroo organizers always deliver a fantastic lineup. Once you survive four days sleeping outside and watching awesome bands in the intense Tennessee heat, no one will doubt your festival authenticity. In the world of festivals, getting your Bonnaroo chops makes you legit.

Bonnaroo shows us that sometimes it's not just about the music or the product at hand but rather about finding a way to combine collective passions to reimagine what joy can look like. By blending musical goodness with the adventures in the outdoors, Bonnaroo shows us the role that fusing consumer interests can play in eliciting brand engagement.

Music Festivals Go Global

Music festivals are not just an American phenomenon but have gone global, inviting the world into the joyful, collaborative celebration of shared passions. Here are a few of the more notable festivals around the world.

ROCK AL PARQUE

South America's largest rock music festival attracted crowds of 266,000 over three days in 2010. The festival, held in Bogota, Columbia, celebrates rock music from all over Latin America and is renowned for hosting local rock bands and promoting Colombian rock music.

Rock al Parque demonstrates the power of brands bringing people together through a hyperlocal approach that highlights the creativity of the region. By showcasing the wonders of a single area, the DIT revolution celebrates local glory, using the festival model not only to showcase the creativity of a region around one core passion but to fuel further creative innovation by inspiring a sense of togetherness.

TIJUANA STREET OPERA FESTIVAL

The eleventh annual Street Opera Festival (Festival de Opera en la Calle) extended its duration by a week in 2014 and arranged various activities throughout the city in order to reach a greater audience.

The festival is dedicated to bringing opera to all, so the events are free to the public and perfect for children and adults alike.

The Tijuana Street Opera Festival teaches us that festivals can be used to bring attention to the rising hubs of art forms such as opera, while also showcasing the new middle-class citizens driving the rebirth of each region. Festivals can gather people in new international markets on the fast track to becoming tomorrow's economic centers.

Incredible and Edible Festivals

Like music has, food and technology are also emerging as foundations for shared experiences and collaborative group creativity. Food and innovation festivals are popping up everywhere, bringing people together through a common passion for culinary artistry, technological advancement, and the experience of breaking bread and new ground, together.

Listed here are two of the top culinary festivals in the world, which bring together the best in House of We cuisine while showcasing the new rock star chefs, CEOs, and entrepreneurs behind the new global movement of creative collaboration in the food industry.

MAINE LOBSTER FESTIVAL

Serving over twenty thousand pounds of lobster over the course of five days, Maine's Lobster Festival is one of the premier local food festivals. Located in the small coastal town of Rockland, the Maine Lobster Festival celebrates Maine's biggest export by boiling it alive and eating it—delicious. Thousands of volunteers work for eleven months before the event preparing for the upcoming activities. These include a big parade, several cooking contests, the Sea Goddess Pageant, road races, arts and crafts, lobster crate races, and of course lots and lots of eating.

ASPEN FOOD & WINE CLASSIC

Taking place in Aspen, Colorado, every summer, the Food & Wine Classic is one of the most famous food festivals in the world. Made hugely well known by the popular reality television series *Top Chef*, the Classic offers a weekend full of gourmet cooking demonstrations and samplings prepared by some of the top names in the business. Featuring lessons from dozens of world-renowned chefs, wine tastings, and cooking competitions, this event sells out every year. A portion of the proceeds from the ticket sales is donated to the Grow for Good campaign sponsored by *Food & Wine Magazine*. Grow for Good is a nationwide initiative that supports local farms and encourages sustainable agriculture.

Idea Festivals

SXSW (AUSTIN, TEXAS)

One of the early pioneers of the festival economy, SxSW, or simply South By to those in the know, is the best place in the world to uncover new raw talent. SxSW brings together up-and-coming players in the fields of music, entertainment, and business to spend time learning and partying among the rich and vibrantly growing culture of downtown Austin.

Austin is a new home for hipsters and tech stars, and its streets are lined with trendy restaurants and bars serving haute cuisine and of-the-moment libations. The biggest thrill of South By is that it is used as a launching pad for new technology and new artists, making it *the* place to discover tomorrow's rising stars in all walks of life.

SxSW is the embodiment of culture and commerce colliding in ways that not only identify the innovations of the future but also help create them. Brands must understand this combination to succeed in the House of We, and there is no better place to see the phenomenon in play in a collaborative environment than South By.

WE-COMMERCE

OUISHARE FEST

OuiShare Fest, in Paris, is a three-day festival centered on the sharing economy. In May 2015, a thousand people gathered at the Cabaret Sauvage to talk about the future of such movements as collaborative consumption, open source, makers and fab labs, co-working, crowdfunding, alternative currencies, and horizontal governance—movements that are transforming cities, organizations, and civic action everywhere in the world.

Entrepreneurs and social innovators, nonprofit and business leaders, grassroots activists, and public officials from different corners of the globe are all coming together at OuiShare to build and explore a common vision of a collaborative society.

VIVID SYDNEY

Vivid Sydney is an annual outdoor cultural event boasting immersive light installations and projections, performances from local and international musicians, and an ideas exchange forum featuring public talks and debates from leading creative thinkers.

The event is held annually during winter in the Southern Hemisphere over the course of three weeks in May and June. For eighteen days, creative practitioners, corporate professionals, families, and people of all generations can experience

Sydney's mild winter weather and engage with a truly spectacular event.

The main foci of Vivid Sydney are the multimedia interactive light sculptures and projections that transform various buildings and landmarks in and around the Sydney central business district and harbor into an outdoor nighttime canvas of art.

Billed as the festival where art, technology, and commerce intersect, Vivid has positioned Sydney as the creative hub of Australia and the Asian-Pacific region and delivers both exciting live entertainment and artistic inspiration on a grand scale.

Vivid Sydney has become a must-attend event on the international creative calendar. In 2012, the *Guardian*, a UK newspaper, called it "One of the top 10 ideas festivals in the world—a real brainy break." Vivid Sydney invites, the people of Sydney and visitors from around Australia and the world to enjoy an array of interactive and immersive lighting experiences, live performances, and inspiring ideas.

THE FESTIVAL FOR SOLIDARITY & COOPERATIVE ECONOMY

Taking place every October in Athens since 2012, the Festival for Solidarity & Cooperative Economy is a meeting point not only for groups and people who participate in solidarity and cooperative economy initiatives but also for visitors who are looking for an alternative and sustainable way to live. It is a good opportunity for groups to connect and share knowledge and for visitors to learn and implement new good practices.

The festival is self-organized and self-managed through the collective efforts of roughly two hundred participating groups. The event is centered on the concept of participatory democracy.

EPILOGUE:
WHAT LIES AHEAD

Over the last several years, we have seen experiences trumping products more and more in consumer preferences. Brands that could provide day-to-day offerings that extended beyond the immediate benefit of their product or service were able to stand out in a sea of commodification.

As the world unites in pursuit of a common good that rewards the many over the few, the idea of creating experiences that elicit pure emotion surrounding the core values of peace, empathy, love, and joy will become the fundamental business competency of the age. At this juncture, despite all of the global strife we are currently witnessing, the trends of our economy point toward a coming global age of cooperation, understanding, and collaboration.

The further we move away from the collapse of 2008, the further we will move away from a world powered by money and toward one powered by shared experiences. With the democratizing power of technology, which offers everyone a voice and a chance to express themselves, pride in creation will become our first priority, and the success that comes along with it . . . well, it will just come.

Here are my broad-stroke forecasts for the years ahead. You can use them as a road map for your brand in order to strategize your next successful ventures in the world governed by the new laws of We-Commerce:

We will emphasize quality over quantity and be dedicated to art rather than speed. Commerce for commerce's sake is no longer acceptable. Anything put into the world for a profit must find a way to give back to society in kind and to beautify, enhance, and interpret its community and environment.

Collaborative commerce will reduce costs through shared infrastructures. The principles of We-Commerce will apply as much to how things are conceived, created, and produced as to how they are experienced and enjoyed. In the future everything from office space to servers will be shared with an eye to improving efficiency and promoting creativity and collaboration.

Brands and consumers will continue to come together to form a more cohesive and fluid business ecosystem. When you combine crowdfunding platforms, collaborative consumption portals, and community hubs, the whole framework for conducting commerce starts to shift. Rather than being driven by competition in a top-down fashion, commerce is being initiated by the community from the bottom up based on real needs. The new era of business is about creating enterprises that work together in tandem to drive commerce that matters. Instead of buying a cheap, mass-produced product from an unknown manufacturer across the world, people can seek out great products from the people they know best and reestablish trust in the business environment. Technology has enabled the connections to form; now it's time for the next generation to capitalize on them.

The regulatory environment will catch up to the business environment and the sharing economy will then truly take hold. As new models of business predicated more on access than ownership take shape, the rules of engagement will need to change on both a state and federal level to reflect this new environment. Entrepreneurialism will flourish and as a result new industries will continue to appear daily. Consequently, laws that view certain behaviors like renting and leasing as prohibitive will need to be reviewed, with more pertinent regulations appearing in their place.

Customer service will emerge as a critical function from inception. Tomorrow's winning brands will not only have a plan A, based on the product they are offering, but also a plan B, designed to offer a heightened "rescue" component or experience as part of the package. This means including back-up chargers on cellphones or video valets to guide online shopping experiences in case anything goes awry. Immediacy is also part of the rescue package.

Customer-centric companies like Amazon offer options such as a Mayday Button to hit if anything sours your retail experience. The common thread of each of these add-on features and plans is that we are seeing brands respond in ways that are designed to elicit emotion, in this case love, trust, and reliance.

How companies are owned will shift to a cooperative ownership model, with profits in the hands of the many, rather than the few. Companies will be created with an eye toward inspiring positive community experiences while also bringing creativity into commerce's purview. More people will own their own small companies, or invest in them through movements like Slow Money, and work together toward a common good.

It will become more and more acceptable to choose passion and play over work. The trend will be to become a chief engagement officer of your own life. The only thing that matters in today's environment is finding a way to forge connections that lead to deeper and more meaningful paths to profitability, whatever those may be.

Newly enlightened families and individuals will come together in communities defined by their ideals. People will seek places where goods are locally and communally grown and where the craftsmanship of community members supports the community.

Consumers will rally together to bring justice to Main Street and businesses will work to succeed for Wall Street by taking on the responsibility of profiting

only with purpose. As a result brands will become much more than purveyors of goods—they will also be purveyors of *good.*

Brands will emerge as publishers and creators of content rather than just as purveyors of goods and services. For instance, some health insurance companies now offer online counseling or health and wellness programming and literature that their customers might have otherwise gone to magazines to find. This makes them more attractive to their consumers because they are publishing their own content for the benefit of their specific communities and constituencies.

We will be less tethered to technology and more empowered by the freedom it provides, making us less isolated and more communicative. As a result, the worlds of the physical and digital will increasingly coalesce.

Wearables, such as the smartwatch, will take over every part of the landscape, infiltrating industries ranging from technology to health to retail. Wearables will also be one of the first industries to be driven forward by celebrity brand entrepreneurs. Gwyneth Paltrow (Goop), Jessica Alba (the Honest Company), Ellen DeGeneres (Halo), and a litany of other rising, celebrity brands will leverage this new area of technology, which is in essence the next phase of the website or app, to lead the way forward.

Stories will become a critical part of leading business models. Recent successful storytelling strategies include Chipotle creating its own TV series and then hiring renowned authors to adorn their packaging, and New Balance launching an author series that differentiates its sneakers not through designs or colors but through narratives about notable characters that elicit emotion. These stories, just like the fables of old, are the vessels that will unite consumers through feeling; brands that tell their stories well will increase their followers' emotional investment.

Women will take their moment on the global stage. After an uncomfortable alliance between the sexes—with women mimicking traditional masculine power relations to get ahead in a man's world—we are now witnessing the emergence of the new woman. Many women are now better educated than their male counterparts. Already, there are more female than male entrepreneurs, and these women inspire others around the globe and have influence across culture and class. This phenomenon is best showcased in the newly anointed trend of betapreneurialism, which is interestingly being driven forward largely by women.

Currently, only 30 percent of European entrepreneurs are women, but by 2020 in advanced economies, two in three graduates will be female, so their contribution will change the landscape of small business. This new movement will make the idea of "leaning in" obsolete as power women realize it is in leaning *out* that the pathway to success is found.

Sound will emerge as the new language. It will be the canvas of ultimate experience. Just as Instagram made pictures the artistic vehicle of the day, the infusion of sound immersion will lead to a wave of innovation in the audio realm. The sound wearable category will prove to be the tip of the iceberg, with music experiences being reimagined through various streaming radio offerings and other custom delivery vehicles that will showcase new ways to appreciate great sound. Just as we saw the big stars flee the big screen with the fall of the movie industry, which led to a TV renaissance and the phenomenon of binge TV, the same thing will happen with sound. Radio will be reconstructed. Concert-going experiences will become more infused with feelings of festival, community, and utopia. And the idea of binge radio isn't too far away as a result. The future will definitely be as much about what you hear as what you see.

The shift from me to we that is occurring at every level in our culture and current we-conomy has the potential to provide for the vision of a global village that the idealistic society of the 1960s dreamed of but could never manage to implement. With today's technology, the utopian hopes of that last age of creative destruction can, with proper stewardship, be realized, along with the best values of that era: peace, love, ecology, freedom of expression, and responsible business practices, along with an economy based on quality, shared abundance, justice, and a reverence for the earth.

Here's to hoping that we can all collaborate, using the principles in this book, and co-create a better We-Commerce world together, for the good of the many rather than the few.

AFTERWORD

WE-CONS ON WHAT'S COMING UP IN THE WE-CONOMY

Throughout the course of writing this book, I came across many pioneers whom I view as icons—they redefine the face of culture and commerce through their unique perspectives on the world and business. I have come to think of these individuals as We-cons, the voices of a new We-Commerce who can be heard in every sector today from food and media to fashion and philanthropy. Together they are blazing a trail toward a new future, and so I have asked a few of them to weigh in on what they think is coming up next.

FRANK ROSE ON THE FUTURE OF MEDIA

Frank Rose is an award-winning author and senior fellow at Columbia University in New York City. Frank was among the first to recognize the age of immersion that would drive We-Commerce by marrying the physical and digital worlds in groundbreaking ways. Here's what Frank had to say about the future of media and big advertising.

The media industry today is totally different, and still changing in ways that can't entirely be predicted. Advertising as we've known it is clearly not going to survive, and that puts all ad-supported media at risk. And media is becoming participatory in ways that most denizens of industrial-age mass media are never going to truly understand. So the economic basis and the product itself are both changing utterly. The good news is that we get to reinvent the way we communicate with one another in a way that we haven't been able to in 180 years. The bad news is there's going to be a lot of chaos until we get there. Though maybe that's good news too? This is the central question of our time. Digital media. Virtual reality. Artificial intelligence. The boundaries are blurring—and they're not going to get any clearer.

During the summer of 1966, Andy Warhol did a series of interviews with Gretchen Berg that were published in the East Village Other, *and Andy said, "I don't know where the artificial stops and the real starts." It's generally considered the best interview he ever did, though eventually it came out that his words were heavily edited and even combined with the questions, so that what he was supposed to*

have said was very smooth and quotable and what he actu-
ally said was kind of bland. Which of course is very Andy.

Andy said (or didn't say) a lot of great things in this inter-
view, but [the quote above] is my favorite. He was talking about
his films, but as a general observation it's brilliant. I mean, who
does know? What is artifice? What is real? They're so mixed
up it's impossible to tell. And he was talking in the 1960s, when
artifice was still a cottage industry compared to what it is now.

JASON KRANTZ ON THE FUTURE OF FOOD

Jason Krantz is the executive chef at Jacob's Pickles in New York City. He is a culinary artist dedicated to using food as a gateway to expression. Whether he's mastering the plethora of experiences that can be created through the art of pickling or telling stories through the flavor profiles he uniquely curates with sauces and fresh spins on traditional cuisines, Jason is a true collaborator and innovator in the world of fine dining. Here's what he had to say about the future of food.

Today, the spectrum of the lens on food has changed; it has sharpened, brightened. And that lens is now available to everyone to look through and decide: where do we go from here? I think one of the biggest trends I see in food today and going forward is hospitality. Hospitality is a state of being and an extension of oneself. The hospitality is what magnifies the experience of the craft and thought of food.

AFTERWORD

If I looked back eighteen years ago to where and how I was going to cook I would have explained differently. For me it was always about executing at the highest level of integrity of what I can do. The integrity hasn't changed, but it's more the ability to reach many rather than the few.

Before it was all about fine dining; now it's about what is soul satisfying, gratifying, and how people can still enjoy without be confined economically. Food is more of an emotional and intellectual state of being. It is a heightened awareness of what, where, when, with whom, and how we eat.

TAMMY TIBBETS ON THE FUTURE OF SOCIAL GIVING

Tammy Tibbets is the founder and president of She'sTheFirst, which is a revolutionary nonprofit dedicated to raising funds to send a first generation of women to college around the world. Tammy has used her insights and intellect to reimagine what both nonprofits and education can look like, and in doing so, has empowered new generations of women to make a difference. Here's what Tammy had to say about what's next in social giving in the new we-conomy.

The effective start-ups in the nonprofit world today are resourceful and leverage creative marketing and storytelling just like the big brands do with their megamillion advertising, but we do it without the red tape and bureaucracy slowing us down. Social media platforms will increasingly give us the foundation to aggregate the small actions of individuals into a large movement. People want to share what makes them happy and what makes them look savvy with others, and that is only going to continue to grow. The millennial generation is so committed to social good. So by taking a bottom-up, community-driven approach—crowdsourcing ideas and prototyping faster to make sure that the solutions they are proposing actually meet the needs—all approaches will become increasingly important for not-for-profits in the future.

CARRIE HAMMER ON THE FUTURE OF FASHION

Carrie Hammer is one of the first designers to offer bespoke tailoring for women in business. She has used her company to usher in a new fashion aesthetic and new definitions of beauty. Carrie's use of role models as opposed to runway models in all of her shows is both innovative and inspirational, transforming both the women's apparel business as well as the lives of many of her consumers. Here is what she had to say about the future of fashion.

Women *shop online. Period. Sure there will always be stores, but we are moving all of our consumer behavior online and it's fascinating. We eventually will have fit and customization tools that will deliver custom clothing to our homes within minutes via 3-D printing machines.*

As technology changes at such a rapid pace, we need to make sure we keep ahead of our competition and new entrants to the marketplace. Not only is there no longer a first mover's advantage; I believe there is actually a first mover's disadvantage. If you don't keep evolving creatively, new entrants can copy and use their cash reserves to iterate faster than you.

We are now in a sharing and collaborative economy. We have never been closer together and yet so geographically far apart. We can work from every corner of the world in the most collaborative ways.

JESSIE HEMMONS (ISHKNITS) ON
THE FUTURE OF ART + COMMERCE

Jessie Hemmons is a public fiber artist, or yarn bomber, who uses her knitting to cover objects in public spaces in order to offer viewers a new way to perceive and interact with their everyday world. Jessie's objective is to be a positive influence on her environment, whether it be through the use of artwork for branding and commercial opportunities or through working with community youth to inspire them to find their creative vision. Here's what ishknits had to say about the evolving relationship between street art and commerce.

Right now, we are in the midst of a historic shift in the way that businesses treat their employees and their customers, and I'm very excited to be an active participant in that change. My artwork is inspired by the consumer. My mission as an artist is first to amuse and entertain and second to engage the viewer in understanding that our urban spaces can be used for collaborative creativity. I think that larger businesses that commission my work have an understanding of how I interact with my audience and want to be a part of that process, and I see this trend continuing in the future.

Street art has shifted from "anti-establishment" to becoming more and more part of the mainstream. People don't necessarily see it as a nuisance, and that means that artists have had to adjust their work to fit this shift. I've seen work become more entertaining and engaging rather than shocking or political. I fell in love with street art for its original rebelliousness and angst. New generations of street artists are starting to appreciate its value as part of mainstream culture, and it has inherently changed the work. It has also changed the role of the artist.

Artists have generally tried to disrupt the status quo and shock us out of complacency. Today, artists becoming businesspeople is no longer taboo. If your art is used for business purposes, you're no longer necessarily a "sell-out." Now, it's more like, how was your art used and how can you use your art to progress your ideas for change? I think art can be used as a means to an end more than an end in itself.

CHRISTINE OSEKOSKI ON THE FUTURE OF
SOUND AND THE WE-CONOMY

Christine Osekoski is the former publisher of *Fast Company* magazine and current executive vice president for Katz Media Group. Both in print and now radio, Christine is a true disruptor, taking her brands way beyond the pages of a magazine, with marquee events and salon dinners feteing the A-list. Her content bridges the gap between digital and physical and is reinventing publishing and, more recently, sound.

Being *the publisher of* Fast Company *for the last eight years provided real insights into the we-conomy. With the birth of Facebook and Twitter, social media exploded and grew into being a part of everyday, minute-by-minute life. Facebook democratized content curation and provided an environment for real-time conversations to begin bringing strangers around the world closer and giving consumers and citizens a voice to which businesses, marketers, and governments would have to pay attention. Soon thereafter other social media followed as did apps like Yelp and Urban that allowed consumers to share their reviews. This new sharing economy paved the way for other businesses like Airbnb, TaskRabbit, and Lyft. Consumers, too, were collaborating on giving to charities, supporting causes, and helping small businesses get funded.*

AFTERWORD

Larger businesses of real scale are now trying to mimic some of these game-changer start-ups, altering their own strategies in favor of what the consumer is choosing. I foresee the sharing and collaborative we-conomy moving forward, not backward. Yet I also see some of the new models looking back to the old ones that have managed to stay alive and successful. For example, while music streaming services are nouveau, they (Spotify, Pandora, and Beats 1) are looking back and taking cues from the oldest medium, radio. Why? Because sometimes the old models simply work—and it proves that we can learn from our past, present, and future.

ACKNOWLEDGMENTS

Many people past and present have guided me in the creation of this work and I'd like to express my gratitude here.

A very special thanks to Bev West for helping me write this book. I couldn't have told the story I was trying to tell without her guidance and the benefit of her decades of experience and insight as an author. Thanks to her as well for helping me take a very broad approach and transform it into accessible information that's relevant to readers.

I'd also like to thank the incomparable Joe Veltre from the Gersh Agency for believing in my vision and getting my first book sold. Joe, I wouldn't be here without you, and I am so appreciative for all.

Deep gratitude to Jeanette Shaw, my editor at Perigee, for her vision, patience, and guidance throughout this process. You have been invaluable.

Thanks also to my first boss, the late Aimee Laurel, for

giving me my first shot and introducing me to the world of media relations I have built my career upon.

Deepest love and appreciation to my second boss and "mother," the inimitable Diane Perry. She nurtured me both personally and professionally in my formative years and I wouldn't be where I am without her lessons of leadership and love.

Many thanks to Faith Popcorn for allowing me the honor of representing her and changing my life by introducing me to the power of trend forecasting and an intimate knowledge of culture. My entire business has been built on an intersection of culture and commerce and I will always be grateful to her for providing that clarity and perspective.

Tons of love and admiration to my first true industry mentor, the fabulous Diane Gayeski, dean of the Park School of Communications at Ithaca College. Diane was the first to call bullshit on my not always striving to reach my full potential back in 1993 in one of her classes. Thanks to her I have never looked back or doubted the power of my imagination and dreams.

Thanks to Weber Shandwick for my fourteen-plus-year career at the world's leading PR firm. I appreciate the opportunity they gave me to redefine the game of global media relations, and to this day feel blessed having served many of the world's leading companies and senior executives in this capacity.

Gratitude to the two most significant pioneering clients of BRANDthropologie: Fast Company and Alvarez & Marsal.

ACKNOWLEDGMENTS

Christine Osekoski, you have been my wonder twin since the day we met and have done everything from having my back to being the best partner I could ever hope for to innovate with. Thank you my sistah. I can only imagine what is ahead for us.

Rebecca Baker, you saw my potential early on and allowed me to go beyond public relations to help reimagine the possibility of the communications function in its entirety. I am extraordinarily proud of the work we have done together and know without question that it has changed the game.

Thanks to my journalist friends who have always supported me and made me feel like one of the "chosen" few PR people who was truly different.

Frank Rose, I will never forget how you captured the time we first met in my office in your book the *Art of Immersion*. Your impression of me changed my impression of myself and has been invaluable to my journey, so thank you.

Bill Holstein, thank you for co-creating with me for more than twenty years. Whether it has been in your capacity as premiere journalist or colleague, I am extremely proud of the work we have done together, and will always be grateful for all it has imparted to me.

Thanks to everyone gracious enough to share their stories with me . . . Jason, Carrie, Tammy, Frank, Ish, Josh, and Christine. Your perspectives were invaluable and helped me to know that the power of We-Commerce did truly exist.

Deep thanks to all my friends and family who have served as my support system through the good and bad.

ACKNOWLEDGMENTS

Iris, Arnie, Mitchell, Cora, Jonathan, Laura, Jen, Bev, Kimberly, Lisa, Randi, Amy, Margo, Christine, Maureen, Gwen, Allyson, Jason, Ric, Josh, Gordon, Ali, Dawn, and countless others . . . I couldn't have reached this moment without the love and strength of you all. Thank you.

To Maddie and Harvey. While it was difficult to walk together in life, I feel you guiding me each day from where you are now. Thank you for all that each of you gave to make me who I am.

To the most precious and beautiful soul I know . . . thank you to my baby Bugsy Morrison Howard. You made me believe in love again and gave me back my heart and soul as a result. I love you beyond words.

And last, to my love and best friend Ned . . . thank you for loving me just as I am and just as you do. Success wouldn't be as sweet as it is if I didn't have you to share it with.